Helion & Company Limited
Unit 8 Amherst Business Centre
Budbrooke Road
Warwick
CV34 5WE
England
Tel. 01926 499 619
Email: info@helion.co.uk
Website: www.helion.co.uk
Twitter: @helionbooks
https://helionbooks.wordpress.com/

Cover: A soldier of the KPA poses with a Type 73 GPMG at an undisclosed location in 2013. (AFP)

Designed and typeset by Mach 3 Solutions (www.mach3solutions.co.uk)
Cover design Paul Hewitt, Battlefield Design (www.battlefield-design.co.uk)

ISBN: 978-1-915070-62-3

British Library Cataloguing-in-Publication Data
A catalogue record for this book is available from the British Library

CONTENTS

ABBREVIATIONS AND ACRONYMNS

AA	anti-air
AAA	anti-aircraft artillery
AFV	armoured fighting vehicle
AGL	automatic grenade launcher
APC	armoured personnel carrier
ATGM	anti-tank guided missile
C4ISR	command, control, communications, computers, intelligence, surveillance and reconnaissance
DMZ	Demilitarized Zone
DoD	Department of Defense (US)
DPRK	Democratic People's Republic of Korea
ERA	explosive reactive armour
GDP	gross domestic product
GPS	Global Positioning System
GPMG	general-purpose machine gun
HE	high explosive
HEAT	high explosive anti-tank warhead
IIR	imaging infrared
KCBC	Korean Central Broadcasting Committee
KCNA	Korean Central News Agency
KPA	Korean People's Army
KPAAF	Korean People's Army Air and Anti-Air Force
KPAGF	Korean People's Army Ground Force
LRF	laser rangefinder
LWR	laser warning receiver
MANPADS	man-portable air-defence system
MBT	main battle tank
MCLOS	manual command to line of sight
MRL	multiple rocket launcher
NLL	Northern Limit Line
NLOS	non-line-of-sight
ROK	Republic of Korea [South]
ROKA	Republic of Korea Army [South]
RPG	rocket-propelled grenade
SACLOS	semi-automatic command to line of sight
SMG	submachine gun
SOF	Special Operations Force
SPG	self-propelled gun
UAV	unmanned aerial vehicle
UN	United Nations
US	United States
USA	United States of America
USFK	United States Forces Korea
USSR	Union of Soviet Socialist Republics
WMD	weapons of mass destruction
WPK	Workers' Party of Korea

PREFACE

The DPRK. Shrouded in mysticism and secrecy, the nation represents an absolute unicum for the military analyst. No other country in the world manages to attract so much scrutiny to its controversial antics, yet divulge so little of material importance about its inner workings. This might be at the heart of why this country specifically has gripped our attention for so many years, and drawn us to write this series about its largely mysterious armed forces.

Before we introduce the main subject, a couple of clarifications and disclaimers regarding the contents of this book. Since all claims made represent the latest analysis of current military matters in a country that is notoriously secretive, some are bound to turn out to be incorrect as new information comes to light. Wherever a claim is made that cannot be established with absolute certainty, it is clarified through appropriate qualifiers: plausible, likely, and all variations of like sort. Sources are mentioned for those claims that do not bank on our own work, when they are absent it may be assumed that the claim is either an original finding of the authors or held to be common knowledge.

As the subject we have written on mainly concerns the DPRK (Democratic People's Republic of Korea), it is the North Korean romanisation scheme of Korean that we have attempted to adhere to for most Korean names, which differs from those schemes common in the South. In some cases this might be cause for confusion, further clarification of what exactly is referenced is then usually provided. In similar vein, designations of the Korean People's Army's various branches are matched to their North Korean analogues, abbreviations of which are adopted as follows: Korean People's Army, KPA; Korean People's Army's Ground Force, KPAGF; Korean People's Army Air and Anti-Air Force, KPAAF; Korean People's Army Navy, KPAN; Special Operations Force, SOF; Missile General Bureau, MGB.[1] These branches also serve as the main structure of this book series, and are treated in the order listed above. We'd also like to express our profound gratitude to our dear friend Tarao, whose aid in researching and promoting this project has been indispensable. Furthermore, the variety of talented artists that have contributed to the many wonderful artworks deserve nothing but praise.[2] Any questions on this publication or related matters are more than welcome, and may be directed to onthepathofsongun@outlook.com.

A map of North Korea with the most important locations mentioned in the volume. (Map by George Anderson)

INTRODUCTION

Tuesday, 2:34PM (GMT+9), 23 November 2010

Supposedly responding to a South Korean artillery exercise which targeted waters across the Northern Limit Line (NLL), a battery of six 122mm multiple rocket launchers (MRLs) and possibly a number of 76mm coastal defence artillery pieces fires a devastating barrage upon Yeonpyeong Island. Occurring on 23 November, the surprise attack was conducted in the same year as the ROKS *Cheonan* sinking, and caught the Republic of Korea Army (ROKA) units stationed on the island completely unawares. Much of the seven square kilometre island burned down in the resulting carnage, and two military, as well as two civilian, lives were claimed (North Korean casualties from return fire remain uncertain). Extensive preparations to the artillery exchange, including the redeployment of the offending MRL battalion on the adjacent Kangnyong Peninsula, the setting up of a secure land communications line to this unit and the mobilisation of several other assets, including a flight of five MiG-23 fighter aircraft, in the hours preceding the attack, are all indicative of the deliberate prior intent of the attack. Furthermore, the characteristics of the rocket launch itself similarly implied a well-prepared and calculated provocation, refraining from escalating with heavier barrages while the artillery power to do so was present in abundance.[1] South Korean artillery swiftly initiated return fire (though it was later deemed to be largely inaccurate as a direct result of North Korean jamming of the AN/TPQ-37 weapon-locating radar), to which a smaller second bombardment was conducted in answer.[2]

Some have claimed the Yeonpyeong bombing was conducted in response to a South Korean artillery exercise which supposedly targeted waters across the NLL, but in truth the incident fits into the larger context of North Korean provocations that have typified its aggressive foreign policies since its founding. These planned provocations often serve as the basis for the rise to power of an important figure within the Workers' Party of Korea (WPK) or KPA, or otherwise are conducted for symbolic reasons, to prove loyalty, or even simply as an act of revenge. As anticipatory measures the DPRK nowadays usually mobilises fighter aircraft, air-defence systems and anti-ship missiles in the general vicinity of where a resulting confrontation might take place. In committing acts that fall short of outright triggering a war, the DPRK has been able to seriously influence its neighbours, and in the least retain its place in the international spotlight given that its economical and political influence are nowadays insufficient to do so. The potentially colossal humanitarian and financial catastrophe brought on by the onset of full-scale hostilities has in the past often been enough to discourage the Republic of Korea (ROK) and USA from retaliating militarily, though only through exercising great restraint. Provocations such as these, whether they occur close to the DMZ or even in entirely different nations, are the staple of inter-Korean relations and provide a stark reminder of the fact that a renewed conflict is never far away. Given that the economical and technological situation in the two Koreas are nowadays more in contrast than any two bordering countries in the world, the reason why this threat remains so potent might be obscure to some. However, despite the fact that in the past decades the KPA has suffered much in terms of technological prowess and overall upkeep relative to its Southern neighbour, in considering its current strength its ability to import weapons and technology from abroad (especially before the sanctions regime) is often underestimated, and the capabilities of its indigenous military industry even more so. Some of these acquisitions lean on old relations with like-minded governments, others simply exploit the black market; others still are of surprising sophistication, and suggest some larger geopolitical game is at play, presumably motivated by a Russian and Chinese desire to uphold North Korea's status as a buffer zone between these countries and Western-aligned South Korea. It is the latter category that has allowed the DPRK to reverse engineer or otherwise copy sensitive weapons systems and technologies such as the S-300 air-defence system, Kh-35 anti-ship missile and an advanced 300mm multiple rocket launcher, not to mention a myriad of developments related to its ballistic missile programme. In more recent years, the pace at which new designs, sometimes with a clear foreign influence, at other times entirely original, have appeared is unmatched even by some major powers. Research, development and particularly the production of these systems (often within short timeframes) by the North Koreans is impressive, potentially indicative of an outside influence that has aided them. Whatever the case, it has not only enabled a revival of the KPA as a fighting force, but also helped keep the DPRK's military exports competitive during an age of ever-tightening sanctions. North Korean arms stemming from the past half-century remain abundant across the globe, and as it produces (or formerly produced) many of the weapons systems Soviet-aligned nations were supplied with, it is a source of affordable maintenance and upgrades. Its efforts at keeping these – now illegal – exports a secret constitute some of the toughest challenges to the United Nations (UN) in dealing with the nation, each year spawning extensive investigations and expansions of sanctions. Were it not for the unrelenting pressure exerted on other UN members to adhere to the embargoes in place, North Korea would likely be a major arms exporter, generating much revenue for a state known for its economic hardship, as well as allowing it to regain some of the influence decades of isolation have bereft it of. Of course, the days where the DPRK could boast of substantial economic gains and widespread political clout have long gone. In an age then where its adversaries enjoy a massive technological and economical advantage, and its traditional allies for the first time show hesitation in their resolve, the KPA Ground Forces face an unclear future. Will they wither in the shadow of North Korea's blooming nuclear arsenal, or will stubborn adherence to the Songun (military first) doctrine allow them to soldier on?

1
KOREAN PEOPLE'S ARMY GROUND FORCES

Great powers typically upkeep massive armies for self-defence or protection of their interests abroad. As a rule, those possessing the largest populations or most prosperous economies correspond with being able to sustain the largest armed forces. This is just the first point at which the KPA stands out like a sore thumb amongst its peers. With a population of some 26 million and a GDP that only escapes derision by the difficulty in its estimation, its standing forces compete with the absolute top contenders on the international stage in terms of active personnel. This vast military apparatus has over the years resorted to a variety of curious tactics to supply its forces with a correspondingly excessive amount of equipment, the result of which has generally not been favourable to its international image. Nonetheless, its efforts at maintaining a force of this size have been anything if not realistic, and they are the sole reason its operational capabilities are not to be underestimated even after decades of what could be perceived as stagnation. In fact, on the technological front the KPA's Ground Forces are undergoing one of the largest upheavals since their foundation, albeit as yet on a relatively limited scale.

Before discussing modern day developments however, it is worth painting an accurate picture of its origins, which helps to explain some of the unique characteristics exhibited by the KPA. The DPRK actually celebrates two separate founding dates, the first referring to the foundation of a resistance army against the Japanese, retroactively named the Korean People's Revolutionary Army, on 25 April 1932, and the second as the modern KPA on 8 February 1948.[1] Although it is the former that has been incorporated in the flags of the various military branches, the second has been once again acknowledged in recent years and celebrated since 2018 as well. This peculiar duality in its foundations is reflected even in the modern-day tactics employed by the modern KPA, stressing the importance of guerrilla warfare and the creation of a 'second front' in South Korea alongside conventional large scale operations. These large scale operations would likely still much resemble the ones conducted during the early stages of the Korean War, with North Korean doctrines focussing on a blitz-type attack with the aim of swiftly decapitating the South Korean army and occupying the South.

Of course, such planning also has to take into account the vast changes that have occurred since the Korean War, or the Fatherland Liberation War as it is known in the North. Triggered by the division of Korea after the end of the Second World War, tensions between the communist-backed regime of the North led by Kim Il Sung and that of the South under Syngman Rhee led to an open invasion of the South on 25 June 1950. Although the consensus is that the invasion – which was extensively planned prior to this date – commenced with a North Korean offensive, clashes along the 38th Parallel that divided the two sides had been initiated frequently by either side and the North Korean narrative remains that the South attacked first.[2] With an army both quantitatively and qualitatively superior to the ROKA Kim Il Sung managed to take Seoul in just two days and destroy the majority of opposing forces in under a week. Caught off guard by the invasion, the US response through the UN was unable to halt the North Korean offensive, often lacking appropriate armament to counter the North's armour which it had received from the Soviet Union in the buildup before the war. By August all that was left was a small pocket around the south-eastern city of Pusan where the overextension of the North Korean supply lines and extensive bombing led to a stalemate that would hold for over a month before KPA forces were all but exhausted. Subsequent landings of troops at Inchon near Seoul led to the recapture of the capital and the decimation of retreating KPA forces, followed by the capture of Pyongyang on 19 October and much of the North's territory. This prompted China, under strong encouragement of Mao Zedong, to dedicate its newly designated People's Volunteer Army (PVA) into the fight, fighting back UN forces to beyond the 38th Parallel through a series of massive offensives which essentially sidelined the KPA's and, by extension, Kim Il Sung's role for the rest of the war. Although still hesitant to directly involve itself, the Soviet Union also stepped up its efforts and began flying sorties over Chinese-held territories, further escalating the war with the first large scale jet-on-jet aerial engagements. On the ground, the PVA and UN forces slowly entered into a deadly stalemate along the 38th Parallel, where fighting first erupted. After reconquering Seoul in January 1951, a setback which infamously led General MacArthur to consider the use of nuclear weapons, the city traded hands a fourth time just over two months later, leaving it completely in ruins. After June however, the front remained almost entirely stable for another two years, while sporadic efforts at negotiating an armistice did little to diminish the intensity of a series of battles and the continuous aerial bombardment of targets in the North. With both sides coming to the realisation that a breakthrough was nowhere in sight, a Korean Armistice Agreement was reached on 27 July 1953, detailing the cessation of hostilities until a final peaceful settlement is achieved, as well as the creation of the Korean Demilitarized Zone (DMZ). This heavily monitored border area continues to divide the two Koreas to this day as a final peace treaty never materialised – meaning that they have technically remained at war ever since. Although much of the Korean Peninsula was practically razed to the ground through years of fighting with negligible territorial gains by either side as a result, the DPRK still considers the outcome a victory, and celebrates 27 July as Victory Day. Of course, this may be influenced by the fact that it adheres to a completely different narrative about the course of the Korean War, with wildly diverging statistics pertaining to the amount of lives and equipment lost on either side. The total number of UN military casualties is put at 1,567,128, of which 405,498 were 'US imperialist soldiers of aggression' – close to three times the numbers reported by the US Department of Defense (DoD).[3]

The freshly established Korean People's Army, despite having been built up and consequently almost entirely destroyed during the war, still came out of the fighting better equipped and organised than it had ever been. Initially supported by hundreds of thousands of Chinese forces, by the end of the 1950s the KPA stood mostly on its own legs, numbering some 350,000 personnel and inheriting advanced equipment mainly from the Soviet Union. Nonetheless, it was now actually outnumbered by the ROKA, which albeit lacking in modern equipment and hampered by economic difficulties, managed to upkeep a standing army of some 650,000.[4] Although modernisation of its branches during the 1950s and 60s ensured it maintained a thin technological edge, this situation mainly persisted in the direct post-war era. The status quo shifted when, in the late 1960s and 1970s, the KPA entered a defining period, one that would

A North Korean armoured formation of the 105th Tank Division equipped with T-34 tanks and SU-76 self-propelled guns enters Seoul on the 27th of June 1950, just two days after the KPA crossed the 38th parallel. (KCBC)

drastically transform its ground forces in size and equipment as well as overall doctrine. In accordance with its newly established Juche (self-reliance) idea, far-reaching efforts were made to dramatically increase military spending and set up an indigenous industry for producing most of the equipment required for its ground forces. Such plans were for instance outlined during the 2nd WPK conference on 5 October 1966 during which Kim Il Sung called for an emphasis on development of the defence industry.[5] Military spending was adjusted accordingly, falling just short of half the total budget, in contrast to the 31.2 percent allotted to the military previously.[6] Although it would take decades before the Songun policy would be officially instituted, the push for modernising its defence industry in the late 1960s and 70s was de facto the first practical instance of it. It is no coincidence that the period immediately following the 1966 conference saw a steep rise in inter-Korean clashes such as the infamous 1968 Blue House raid, 1968 *Pueblo* incident and 1969 EC-121 shootdown, but also many more minor skirmishes resulting in the deaths of hundreds. These years of dramatically increased hostilities have so far been unsurpassed in intensity despite the decades of virtually unabating animosity between the two countries since. Aside from deadly encounters along the DMZ, the period was also the backdrop to numerous infiltrations by the North mainly along the South's coastline, but also including the hijacking of a Korean Air Lines' YS-11 together with its 50 crew members and passengers. Although South Korea responded in kind with raids and incursions into the DPRK, hostilities were primarily instigated by the North in a deliberate campaign aimed at bringing about regime change in the South. The costly operations yielded little success that helped realise such a goal, and hostilities died down again towards the end of 1969.[7] That tensions remained high is attested to by the shootdown of a US helicopter by South Korean forces in 1974, who were anticipating a North Korean raid on the presidential palace.[8]

The drastic increase in military spending and subsequent buildup of the KPA manifested itself in the delivery of thousands of tanks from the Soviet Union and China, including these Type-59 MBTs seen here during a military exercise. (KCBC)

By the early to mid 1970s North Korea was producing increasing amounts of indigenous weaponry as part of its efforts to become self-sufficient. Many components still needed to be sourced from abroad however, and the new policies were leaving clear marks on the stumbling North Korean economy, casting doubt on their effectiveness. Nonetheless, the KPA once again began to take shape as an invasion force, its tactics drawing heavily from experiences gained during the Korean War. Inspired by the success of North Vietnam in capturing the South in 1975 and dismayed at the failure to instigate a revolution through the South Korean populace, it is believed that Kim Il Sung asked China for support in engaging in another war against South Korea.[9] With the Sino-Soviet split, Cultural Revolution and perceived Chinese inaction in the Vietnam War having deteriorated Sino-Korean relations (although they were since on the mend), as well as Mao Zedong's poor health at the time, it is perhaps not surprising that this request was denied. Still, a confrontational attitude continued to typify North Korean policies throughout the 1970s. In fact, in November 1974 the first of four tunnels burrowed directly under the DMZ was found, followed by additional discoveries in 1975, 1978 and 1990. These 'Tunnels of Aggression' often measured more than a kilometre in length, running over a hundred metres deep through bedrock. In effect, they would allow invading forces to circumvent the heavily fortified border area and instantly overtake the ROKA's border guards and vast minefields – a tactic which could potentially have very high payoffs in the initial stages of open hostilities. Another high-profile incident of the 1970s serves to illustrate the mutual animosity and high tensions between the two nations at the time, and is known as the axe murder incident. In this deadly clash over the cutting/trimming of a tree near the DMZ, two US Army officers were killed, with each side accusing the other of starting the fighting. The incident was followed by a tense stand-off between forces at the DMZ while US forces cut the tree down, a carefully measured show of force aimed at displaying resolve without escalating the situation. Even though the incident was likely purely the result of the level of animosity between opposing force at the border, the precariousness of the situation is well illustrated by the fact that Kim Il Sung appears to have genuinely believed the USA planned the incident in advance as a provocation.[10] It is interesting to note that until the mid 1970s, US intelligence vastly underestimated developments undertaken by the North Koreans to modernise and expand their military in the years prior.[11] Assessments of inventory holdings, armoured fighting vehicles (AFVs) and numbers of deployed personnel often diverged from actual values almost by a factor of two, and an invasion could well have caught the DPRK's opponents completely off guard as a result.[12]

The 1970s also brought on a gradual souring in relations between the DPRK and the USSR, caused mainly by Kim Il Sung's policy to attempt to maintain equal relations between China and the Soviet Union after the Sino-Soviet split.[13] Another important factor was North Korea's tendency not to uphold its end of trade agreements and payments and the Soviet Union's resulting reluctance to provide economic aid.[14] The same problem plagued its relations with other traditional allies, the usual explanation provided for which was that the economy was falling short of projections due to the necessity to invest in the defence industry. Thus, while new weapons systems could no longer be comfortably acquired from the Soviet Union, North Korea had now established a capacity to produce equipment in virtually every category for its armed forces. This double-edged sword still reverberates in the DPRK's current economic and military situation, despite having its roots in the policies adopted half a century ago. An additional, historically highly significant reason for the downturn in relations between the DPRK and the USSR is the North's insistence the Soviet Union should aid it in constructing a nuclear reactor for research purposes (a request first filed as early as 1958 and even partially granted, but which only became a true stumbling block in the 1970s).[15] Despite the dearth of deliveries from the Soviet Union between 1975 and 1985, slightly offset by a mending in relations with China starting in the 1970s, the North's ground forces continued to expand gradually into the 1980s until by the end of the Cold War it had transformed into the oversized gargantuan we know it as today. At that point, active forces numbered some 850,000 personnel – an increase of half a million since the end of the Korean War – with reserves coming in at around five million.[16]

The 1983 downing of Korean Air Lines Flight 007 by a Soviet interceptor put a strain on slowly budding relations between the Soviet Union and South Korea for a while, and combined with visits by Kim Il Sung to the Soviet Union in 1984 and 1986 they heralded a period of rapprochement between the two nations. This prompted the Soviet Union to agree to the construction of at least one nuclear reactor and renewed deliveries of advanced weapons systems by the mid 1980s.[17] Although this period was short-lived, for by 1987 the North Korean economy began to falter in earnest and

North Korean ZiL-130 trucks carrying infantry line the road from horizon to horizon in an impressive display of numerical might. (KCBC)

the Soviet Union once again sought to enhance its ties with South Korea, it allowed the DPRK to gain access to new and much-needed military technologies. While the economic turmoil brought on by the fall of the Soviet Union prevented it from applying most of these to its ground forces during the stagnation of the 1990s, efforts were nonetheless undertaken to incorporate them into the indigenous industry. With prospects of a renewed conflict over North Korea's fledgling nuclear programme continuing to trouble the peninsula, the military maintained a slow growth both in size and equipment modernisation. Production of indigenous fighting vehicles persisted commensurately, but at a slower pace than during the massive modernisation efforts of the 1970s and 1980s. In order to ensure the army remained at least superficially at an advantage to the South even through the hardships of the 1990s, including a famine killing hundreds of thousands which was monikered 'The Arduous March' in North Korea, the Songun policy was officially instituted after Kim Jong Il took to power, despite being practically in effect since the 1960s. Regardless, the 1990s and early 2000s mainly constituted a period of decay, during which meaningful production of new weaponry and upkeep of the general armed forces was sidelined for the development of new technologies, including ballistic missile systems. Only after the economy made a slight recovery in the late 2000s, coinciding with the death of Kim Jong Il and Kim Jong Un's takeover at the end of 2011, exercises and military modernisation began once again in earnest.

The development of new weapons systems in the previous decades was consolidated with their actual production, and for a number of years following the adoption of Kim Jong Un's Pyongjin Line policy in March 2013 it appeared the research and development budget was mainly reserved for ballistic missiles and nuclear weapons. Nevertheless, after a moratorium on new designs for the land forces of close to a decade, a virtual flood of ambitious weapons systems was unveiled in the late 2010s and 2020s. With actual introductions seemingly limited to low rate initial production however, it remains to be seen if the technologies involved are not effectively beyond North Korea's grasp. Having inherited a generally technologically outdated, vastly oversized military apparatus from his ancestors, the enigmatic leader is faced with finding solutions to keep the KPA's Ground Forces relevant in an era of tight sanctions, increased threat of nuclear war and direct participation in Russia's conflicts.

2 ORGANISATION

That the leadership is aware of these challenges is a fact surprisingly frankly admitted. For all its self-aggrandising and over-the-top propaganda the KPA is anything if not realistic in its efforts to mitigate them, with Kim Jong Un calling for 'the development of [weaponry] which may outrun the enemies' numerical and technical advantages' on more than one occasion.[1] As Commander-in-Chief of the Korean People's Army,[2] President of the State Affairs Commission, General Secretary of the Workers' Party of Korea and Chairman of the Central Military Commission, Kim Jong Un is in full control and command over every aspect of North Korea's military apparatus. He has the power to direct all elements of the military, and thus also any modernisation efforts aimed at revitalising the Korean People's Army so as to remain a legitimate fighting force in the twenty-first century. In these roles, Kim Jong Un is pictured making visits to units much more often than his father and appears intent on micromanaging affairs for better or worse. As such, he is responsible for sweeping changes in military doctrine and the operational capacity of the KPA as a whole, but also for inspecting whether the paint job on specific aircraft is properly maintained or a new type of equipment that aids in river crossing needs to be developed. As Supreme Leader of the DPRK, Kim Jong Un also oversees a vast political body controlling all aspects of life in the DPRK. The most vital of these is the State Affairs Commission, which is the foremost political organ of the DPRK, and decides upon everything of importance to the country and its course. The State Affairs Commission replaced the National Defence Commission in 2016 to widen its focus on matters other than defence. The President of the State Affairs Commission is elected by North Korea's Supreme People's Assembly (parliament).[3] This of course is a symbolic process only, as the President has always been the leader of the Kim dynasty. The State Affairs Commission comprises the General Staff Department, which exercises command over the whole of the Korean People's Army, as well as the Ministry of National Defence, which is responsible for military diplomacy, construction and military logistics and procurement of arms, munitions and equipment.[4] The Ministry of National Defence's acquisition/production plans are then passed on to the Central Military Commission, which is subordinate to the WPK, which has to formally approve them. Several commands in between link all these organisations together and additional administrational commands further complicate the picture, but these surpass the scope of this volume.[5]

To ensure full political liability of the whole of the KPA and the DPRK, several internal intelligence organs exist that are tasked with maintaining the political ideology of all KPA members, to prevent coups, defections and to look for corruption. These organs serve as the link between the leadership, the WPK and the KPA. The most pervasive ones are the Military-Political Leadership Department and the General Political Bureau, also known as the General Political Department, which are responsible for maintaining the political ideology of the KPA's service people through the deployment of political commissars to army units. The Military Security Command – also known as the Military Security Bureau – is another organ that is tasked with upholding the political ideology of all KPA members and maintains files on all officers, which can be pivotal for the future of their careers. It also searches for corruption and possible attempts to stage a coup within the KPA.[6] Perhaps the most important oversight body of the DPRK is the Organisation and Guidance Department, which is subordinate to the WPK. It conducts surveillance of higher positions such as generals and members of the elite, but also of the General Political Bureau and other intelligence organisations. It grew increasingly prominent under the rule of Kim Jong Il, which used the department to increase his power base while Kim Il Sung was still in power, resulting in it being the top oversight body today.[7] The result of this interleaving network of security agencies is a complex political structure where everyone watches everyone: a necessary property of a police state like North Korea if it is to remain in stasis. While it might seem redundant and in fact highly counterproductive that several organisations could for instance be keeping tabs on the same person, the fact that each organ overlaps in its duties means it is difficult for anyone to gain too much power or influence without it becoming known to others.

Also part of the security apparatus is the Ministry of Social Security, which takes care of the police and civil defence system, including services such as air raid warnings, and the Ministry of State Security. In addition to the latter's focus on military matters, it is also responsible for keeping the population in line, and searches for anything that may harm the state, along with the Ministry of Social Security. Any citizen that is considered to have conducted a political offence is the responsibility of the Ministry of State Security, while the Ministry of Social Security focuses on 'lighter' non-political offences. Together these organisations ensure absolute control over the North Korean population and armed forces.[8] Their ancillary task is to keep high-ranking officials and embassy personnel from defecting, and they work together with the Border Guard Command – also known as Border Guard Bureau – and the Coastal Security Bureau to prevent any illegal entries to, but above all exits out of, the DPRK from occurring. Increasing investment in these particular organs in recent years appears to have had the desired effect, with the number of successful defections sharply dropping since Kim Jong Un came to power.[9] In addition to conducting mass surveillance, both organisations also fill military and auxiliary roles, including the guarding of important facilities. The Ministry of State Security also has elements for foreign intelligence gathering, working alongside the infamous Reconnaissance General Bureau, and is responsible for the security of the Kim family along with the Guard Command: a specialised unit dedicated to the protection of the Kim family and other high-ranking officials, which falls under the control of the State Affairs Commission.[10] Interfering with the lives of simple soldiers all the way up to top ranking officials in the Kim regime, mass surveillance truly plays a central role in the modern KPA, and indeed the DPRK as a whole.

Given the KPA's immense size, such surveillance is indeed a task of gargantuan proportions. With a population of some 26 million, roughly one third of the DPRK's population either serves an active role in the country's military or is part of its reserves and paramilitary forces, despite the fact that its gross domestic product (GDP) per capita is often estimated to be amongst the very lowest in the world. Considering its size and the secrecy surrounding the subject, it is little surprising that the number of active soldiers serving in the KPA is a matter of controversy, with estimates from various sources ranging from roughly 700,000 to 1.2 million.[11] Incorporating its Special Forces, Air Force and Navy branches and considering historical numbers, the total number is likely to be much closer to the second figure however. Being mainly a land-based force, the vast majority of these are ground troops, parts of which are also employed in various non-military roles including agriculture, industry or construction. This provides the North Korean government with a cheap labour force, but obviously also decreases the amount of combat-ready ground forces. During wartime, this army is supplemented by an estimated 7.62 million reserve forces, with additional manpower not yet serving in the active or reserve troops likely to be recruited should the need arise.[12] This intention was attested by North Korea's claim that 3.475 million party members, students, young workers and former soldiers volunteered to join or rejoin the army during a period of heightened tensions between North Korea and the rest of the world due to the advancement of its nuclear weapon programme in 2017.[13] While it is unlikely that this represents the true number of volunteers or even sheer manpower available, it is certainly possible that the KPA could further increase its personnel numbers by recruiting additional forces during times of war. At the same time, there is reason to suggest North Korea is having trouble maintaining its number of active military personnel presumably as a result of the Arduous March, a great famine that took place throughout the late 1990s and decimated a generation – even affecting the average height of North Koreans to this day. Although the food supply has stabilised over the past years, the effects of the Arduous March on North Korea's demographics will be felt for decades to come, and the prospect of another famine remains on the horizon. In recent years, the minimum height and weight requirements have been constantly lowered and have now even practically been abandoned to increase the number of recruits 'fit' for service.[14] The duration of conscription has also continuously been lengthened. Starting with three to four years in the 1950s, this was gradually lengthened until it had reached 10 years in 1993. Although it has remained at this figure, nowadays most males between ages 17 and 30 serve in the military.[15] In addition to lowering the minimum height and weight requirements, some that were previously exempted from conscription are now also required to join. The actual time served depends upon the degree, with university students usually serving for three to five years and those without higher education serving for longer.[16] Some persons are exempted from service, generally those related to high-ranking officials, or those that can utilise their skills to generate foreign revenue for the regime (for instance through hacking activities). Although they usually have to serve for a shorter period of time, an increasing number of women are also conscripted, making up at least partially for the decreased number of men fit for service.[17] Despite conscription starting at 17, basic military training already

North Korean female soldiers manning a 14.5mm ZPU-4 anti-aircraft gun. (KCBC)

A reservist loads a PG-2 grenade into the front end of his RPG-2 anti-tank weapon. Older men like him are unlikely to take part in the initial stages of an invasion of the South, and mainly act as a territorial defence force in case of an invasion of the North. (KCBC)

starts at the age of 14 with the Red Youth Guard. After military service and eventually finishing a full run the military lifestyle still does not end entirely however, as nearly all conscripts that finished their service will go on to join reserve units. All in all, the average citizen is only completely done with military service at the age of 50 or 60, depending on the type of service they did.

These conscripts and reserves serve in an army the organisation of which is subject to continuous reforms. In general, two authorities exercise direct control over the KPA: the General Staff Department and the Ministry of National Defence.[18] Forces under the control of the General Staff Department include the 10 infantry corps (I, II, III, IV, V, VII, VIII, IX, X, and XII), the 91 Capital Defence Corps (formerly known as the Pyongyang Defence Command), one anti-aircraft artillery corps, two tank divisions, four mechanised infantry divisions, seven light infantry divisions, the Special Operations Force, Air Force, Navy and Missile General Bureau.[19 20] The four branches mentioned last will be covered in their own respective volumes. The General Political Bureau has control over the Engineering Corps and the Ministry of National Defence over the Road Construction Corps – formerly known as the Seventh and Eighth General Bureau respectively – after these were reorganised and removed from the oversight of the Ministry of Social Security.[21] In contrast to other countries, the Ministry of Defence has no direct control over combat troops, having gradually lost these powers over the past decades. In total, units from combat brigade level or higher comprise 17 corps and more than 170 divisions and brigades – 89 divisions in total, which are themselves composed of brigades – including 74 infantry divisions (which include the Reserve Military Training Units), two tank divisions, 10 tank brigades, 20 mechanised brigades, 30 artillery brigades, 25 special warfare brigades, 13 strategic missile brigades and 10 brigades serving various purposes in addition to units from other security agencies.[22] As a result of the continuous organisational changes, many old structures are still reported to exist while in fact they do not, and given the pace of these reforms, the structure reported here will become outdated at some point in the not too distant future. Most notably, North Korca is continuously changing corps and division status. The number of corps was the highest during the 1980s and 1990s due to divisions and brigades that had previously been under other commands being brought together into large combined units including four mechanised corps, a single tank corps and two artillery corps.[23] However, the 2000s witnessed a reversal of this policy by shifting some of the assets previously under the command of these corps to the forwards corps stationed closest to the DMZ.[24] The mechanised corps were again reorganised into four mechanised infantry divisions, the tank corps was reorganised as two tank divisions and the remaining artillery corps was incorporated into various (mechanised) divisions.[25] Despite these changes, several of these divisions remain at corps strength, and those located near the DMZ are notably larger than others.

The main component of the KPA's Ground Forces is formed by the infantry corps, of which the I, II, IV and V Infantry Corps are forward deployed near the DMZ in the first echelon. These are larger and equipped with more modern armament and AFVs than the other infantry corps, and utilise large numbers of engineering vehicles, mountain infantry units and light infantry units to allow them to swiftly overcome obstacles that may face them on a southward push. These corps are also reinforced by units of the roughly 620,000 strong Reserve Military Training Units during wartime, enabling an initial attack on the South to draw upon well over half a million soldiers. Still more forces that can be swiftly dedicated to the offensive are located in the second echelon, which consists of the 105th and 123rd Tank Divisions and Mechanised Infantry Divisions. To enable it to rapidly exploit breakthroughs enforced by the first echelon, these forces are the most mobile amongst the KPA and incorporate a large number of AFVs, which are nevertheless still supplemented by large numbers of trucks for the transportation of infantry as opposed to armoured personnel carriers (APCs) or infantry fighting vehicles (IFVs). These two echelons together with a part of the third make up the majority of KPA forces: it is estimated some 70 percent of active ground forces units are stationed south of the Pyongyang-Wonsan line.[26] Additionally, they are frequently strengthened by the redeployment of forces usually stationed deeper inland, such as in the third echelon, which consists of the III and VII Infantry Corps and the 91 Capital Defence Corps. Surrounded by the III Infantry Corps, the 91 Capital Defence Corps is itself similar to a regular infantry corps and works closely together with neighbouring forces to ensure the protection of Pyongyang. The fourth echelon, which is comprised of the VIII, IX, X, and XII Infantry Corps, is located near the border with China, and is presumed to be smaller in size and less well equipped than other forces, serving mainly to protect the strategic rear area and reinforce other echelons when needed.[27] This composition of forces is highly geared towards enabling an invasion that leaves little warning to the DPRK's foes. While war preparations remain necessary, all the equipment, manpower and much of the supplies are already present for a smaller scale war, maximising the element of surprise and denying its enemies the time to bring in reinforcements. A more protracted war would require a far greater and more conspicuous disruption of regular operations for a longer period of time and is in today's climate probably more or less infeasible.

Perhaps the most esteemed and prestigious unit amongst this invasion force is the 'Seoul Ryu Kyong Su Guards 105th Tank Division', which is the KPA's elite tank division, historically operating whatever best equipment could be obtained at the time. Since its tanks are alone in having a chance at successfully engaging ROK and US armour, of which the southern half of the Korean Peninsula knows plenty, this division is of great importance during any push towards the South. Owing the 'Seoul' part of its honorary name to being the first to enter Seoul during the Korean War, its roots trace back to the very first tank unit in the KPA, then commanded by the eponymous Ryu Kyong Su.[28] The use of honorific titles such as these and especially the 'Guards' status is a very common practise within the KPA, and often a multitude are awarded to a single unit. Apart from the use of honorifics, there also exist cover names which are often little descriptive in nature such as the Large Combined Unit 630 for the Special Operations Force or Unit 2625 for one of its SOF battalions, or the 105th Training Centre for the 105th Tank Division. Some of these also incorporate dates of significance in their name,

While war preparations of any country usually see large troop movements closer to the likely conflict zone, an estimated 70 percent of active KPA ground forces are already positioned within close proximity to the DMZ. These units operate equally massive amounts of equipment, such as the dozens of 22-barrelled 240mm multiple rocket launchers seen here. (KCBC)

Kim Jong Un pictured driving a command variant of the Chonma-2 MBT during a military training exercise of the Seoul Ryu Kyong Su Guards 105th Tank Division and other combined tank units of the KPA. (KCBC)

such as the 15th of August Training Centre, further complicating the overall picture.

Aside from the regular armed forces, the aforementioned Reserve Military Training Unit can be quickly mobilised to provide additional manpower. This 620,000-strong reserve unit consists primarily of former conscripts who undergo frequent training comparable to that of active service members.[29] Operating equipment that has been retired by the KPA in the past decades, it can either reinforce an invasion that has been stretched thin or provide protection for the vulnerable coastal areas and strategic rear of the DPRK. Other reserve forces which take longer to mobilise are the Worker-Peasant Red Guard. Numbering some 5.72 million, today this force is equipped mostly with whatever weaponry can be made available for them, including Korean War relics but also a limited amount of more modern armament. This includes artillery and other AFVs; even the venerable T-34 and SU-100 continue service in this reserve branch. The Worker-Peasant Red Guard makes up much of the DPRK population and is as such organised by region and even through specific occupations. It is also responsible for manning many of the DPRK's ubiquitous anti-aircraft artillery (AAA) sites, with villages or factories delegated their own integrated AAA sites, manned by locals and workers. Still more forces are potentially available through the Red Youth Guard. Aged 14 to 16, a force with a potential size of over 940,000 child soldiers undergoing regular training would likely see action during a protracted war (although preparation for military service later in life, not combat, is of course the Red Youth Guard's purpose), owing to the militarised nature of North Korea's society. Other paramilitary units would also come into play during such a war of attrition, providing yet another 340,000+ personnel.[30] The majority of these reserve troops are for defensive purposes only, and supply chains would only be able to sustain a portion of them when deployed in an invasion of the South.

Accompanying its vast numbers of personnel are commensurately large volumes of equipment and fighting vehicles. This includes almost 40,000 pieces of heavy weaponry and armoured vehicles for its ground forces alone, of which roughly 4,300 are main battle tanks (MBTs) and light tanks, 2,600 APCs and IFVs, 8,800 artillery gun pieces (towed and self-propelled, excluding calibres of 76mm and smaller which serve as infantry regiment-level artillery), 5,500 MRLs, 5,000 towed and self-propelled anti-air (AA) pieces, 9,000 fixed AA pieces and 3,000 pieces of equipment for river crossing alone.[31] The figure including equipment held in reserve is even larger, providing the KPA with seemingly endless numbers of fighting vehicles, albeit ones more suited to the battlefields of the Second World War than the combat environment of today.

This force faces some 3.7 million ROK active and reserve troops, reinforced by another 24,000 United States Forces Korea (USFK) troops. Of these, some 625,000 are active Army, Marine Corps, Air Force and Navy troops, with some 490,000 part of the Army.[32] These figures were lowered to approximately 522,000 and 387,000 as part of reforms which aim to raise qualitative standards as opposed to a conventional quantitative structure.[33] These active forces operate roughly 2,200 tanks, 3,100 APCs and IFVs and 5,900 pieces of artillery and MRLs.[34] Although ostensibly much smaller in size to what the KPA can offer, it should be noted that all of these forces would in a North Korean invasion scenario be used on the defensive, and that the KPA will only be able to dedicate part of its forces to offensives in the South, with the majority staying behind in the DPRK. Additionally, ROKA forces generally operate much more and more modern equipment than their Northern adversaries and despite extensive North Korean investment in this area presumably easily outperform the KPA in terms of communications and command structure. Active forces are supported by up to 3.1 million reserve forces, mainly composed of the Mobilisation Reserve Forces, Homeland Reserve Forces and military auxiliaries. Following two years of conscription, another four years of service in the Mobilisation Reserve Forces are typically required, and another four years with the Homeland Reserve Forces after that.[35] As the Homeland Reserve Forces receive little training and equipment, these forces serve mostly to defend strategic rear areas, and are little capable of reinforcing frontline troops should the need arise. The Mobilisation Reserve Forces do receive mobilisation training, meaning almost

Clad in uniforms reminiscent of those worn by Soviet soldiers on the battlefields of Eastern Europe during the Second World War, these Worker-Peasant Red Guards are however armed with the relatively modern North Korean copy of the Soviet AK-74 assault rifle that has begun supplementing Second World War-era weapons like the Mosin-Nagant and PPSh-41. (KCBC)

Towed MRLs like these 122mm 18-tubed launchers are available in high numbers to the Worker-Peasant Red Guard. While these 18-tubed launchers appear to have been built specifically for the Worker-Peasant Red Guard, several other MRL types originally mounted on trucks when still in KPAGF service have since also been placed on simple wheeled carriages to be towed by tractors and civilian trucks, increasing the firepower of reserve forces at no real costs. (KCBC)

1.5 million personnel can be brought (back) into action relatively swiftly. Additional organisations exist for structuring civil defence forces responsible for civilian aspects of military operations during wartime, potentially providing a work force of millions to aid in times of need.[36] Although USFK personnel currently deployed in South Korea number consistently below 30,000, another 50,000 are deployed in neighbouring Japan and thousands more on Guam. Should a war erupt on the Korean Peninsula plans call for the deployment of another 690,000 US ground, naval and air force personnel, although obviously this would take a longer mobilisation time and be heavily dependent on the manner in which the conflict progressed up to that point.[37]

That the DPRK's leadership knows its soldiers are likely to become outnumbered at some point during an invasion is attested by slogans such as 'One Match for a Hundred Foes!'. Although North Korean soldiers are often more experienced than their South Korean counterparts due to their long service, live fire exercises are more seldomly executed in the North, which is especially true for operators of difficult to master equipment such as anti-tank guided missiles (ATGMs). In recent times, efforts have been undertaken to mend this shortcoming with various digital training aids and simulators, but this is generally not a substitute for actual hands-on training with real equipment. One particularly useful aid introduced in 2024 is a system similar to the multiple integrated laser engagement system (MILES), which combines blank cartridges and lasers/laser receivers to accurately simulate combat. Large scale exercises featuring various branches cooperating are held only intermittently however, likely being hampered by fuel shortages. Other exercises are at times less than practical, and more geared towards pleasing the whims of the Kim family and providing propaganda value than preparing troops for actual combat situations. Many also simulate far more practical scenarios however, including for instance mine-clearing and river crossing exercises which prepare KPA troops for the tough terrains they are likely to encounter on their southward push. Regular exercises such as these, as well as keeping a force the size of the KPA organised, armed and combat ready demand a huge budget. Due to the secretive nature of North Korea, the country rarely discloses details of defence spending. In 2014, the Supreme People's Assembly reported that defence expenses took up 15.8 percent of the state's budget, and were set at 15.9 percent for the next year.[38] This allocation has since remained stable. Given the pervasiveness of the military throughout North Korean society and its extensive ballistic missile and weapons of mass destruction (WMD) programmes, it is certain this figure is a vast underestimation of actual expenses however. These are generally estimated to be above 30 percent, and are supplemented by a parallel economy maintained by the Kim family comprising a variety of state companies attempting to earn funds from abroad through illicit means.

North Korean SOF carrying Type-88s adapted to a MILES-type system during exercises in October 2024. Note the smoke generator, marking any hits, on the back of the headwear – a feature found on Chinese analogues of MILES. Nevertheless, the system is believed to be an indigenous development. (KCBC)

Songun-915 main battle tanks of the prestigious 105th Tank Division cross a frozen river during a river crossing exercise. (KCBC)

3
STRATEGY

North Korea's armed forces have two primary objectives: bringing about the reunification of the two Koreas and ensuring the survival of the DPRK and its leadership. To achieve these goals, the KPA uses unique tactics tailored to the Korean Peninsula which draw directly from experience gained observing international conflicts of the past century, the Korean War and even the struggle for independence from the Japanese. Its ability to learn and adapt is essential to maintain any prospect of success in defeating its opposing forces or even keep up a credible deterrent to avoid the DPRK from being targeted or invaded. Whether or not its tactics will ultimately prove to be up to these tasks or not, it is certain that they will present an absolute wild card during wartime, and that a renewed conflict on the Korean Peninsula will be profoundly different from any war waged to this day as a result. By virtue of its long history of staged provocations and even concrete plans for eliciting war, North Korea is often thought of as the future instigator of any conflict on the Korean Peninsula. The DPRK itself however maintains its existence is threatened by US military presence in the region and its hostile policies towards the DPRK, and that peace cannot be attained so long as these factors hold true. Although this sentiment might logically give rise to a militarised society geared towards fortifying the country, the KPA is also uniquely equipped and trained for the offensive role. It is this goal, the goal of reunification, that defines the KPA above all else. Even though the prospect of reunification is now perhaps more distant than it has ever been before (especially under conditions favourable to the DPRK), the KPA remains organised, trained and equipped with this end goal in mind.

Only saved from complete annihilation at the hands of UN forces by China's participation in the Korean War, North Korea spent much of the 1950s and 1960s rebuilding its armed forces and society as a whole, and extensive plans for how to bring about reunification were only laid out in the 1960s. The early foundations for this were the 'Four-Point Military Guidelines' adopted in 1962, calling for:

1. Upgrading the combat efficiency in every possible way
2. Arming all people
3. Fortify the whole country as an impregnable fortress
4. Transforming all soldiers into cadres.[1]

During the 1966 WPK session Kim Il Sung laid out further plans to reunify the Koreas under DPRK rule, in effect one of the first applications of the Songun policy which permeated Kim Il Sung's leadership and practically defined that of Kim Jong Il.[2] Unsurprisingly, these plans saw heavy influence from Kim Il Sung's experiences gained during the Korean War and his actions as a resistance leader fighting against the Japanese. This includes the successes obtained in the early months of the Korean War, but also the stagnation of the invasion at Pusan and the subsequent landings at Inchon which lead to the collapse of the KPA, and the efficacy of guerilla warfare against the Japanese. As such, Kim Il Sung's plans to achieve reunification could be encompassed into three main pillars which are still deemed indispensable for success:

1. A lightning invasion of the whole of South Korea in order to deny US reinforcements landing in territory still in ROK hands, the destruction of infrastructure such as airfields and ports, and by causing large casualty numbers to USFK military personnel dissuading the USA from coming to the ROK's aid.
2. Creating a two-front war by the insertion of large numbers of special forces units in the ROK's strategic rear.
3. Defending the DPRK, and particularly its vulnerable shores against any counter-invasion.

Each of these are important to the point where if one fails, the entire invasion is at risk of failure as well. Although these plans have been constantly modified to incorporate and acknowledge the development of new weaponry and tactics which can either aid or harm their fulfilment, they have remained true to these three pillars in essence to this day.

Although the DPRK has spent much effort in keeping the KPA up-to-date with military (technological) developments around the world, its ability to wage war is closely linked to the current state of politics, which are currently highly unfavourable to North Korea. Starting out with quite explicit support from both China and the Soviet Union during the Korean War-era, and subsequently enjoying a strong backing from both countries throughout much of the Cold War period, relations have now evolved to the point where the DPRK's main value to these two nations is as a buffer zone – and one that brings with it a very high liability. While a mutual aid and cooperation treaty between China and the DPRK was active until 2021, this pact only obligated the nations to come to the defence of the other when one was attacked, and even then China might not have felt it had to adhere to the full implications of the treaty. Indications that China might even take up arms against the DPRK should it be the aggressor in a conflict and the diminishing of the Soviet Union's and then Russia's influence in the region mean that North Korea has little reason to count on any foreign backing at all in a war with the South.[3] A mutual defence pact signed between North Korea and Russia in June 2024 commits both nations to provide immediate military assistance if either is attacked. However, the complete implications of this agreement are still uncertain and may only extend to materiel support. Should one of its traditional allies, particularly China, ever become embroiled in a (direct or proxy) war with the USA in the Asian theatre however, it is highly likely that the DPRK would attempt an invasion so as to force its way into an alliance. This is the only plausible scenario in which North Korea could actually see its goal of reunification on its terms fulfilled, and its prerequisite is ostensibly the advent of the Third World War.

On the other side of the DMZ it is a different story: while US troop numbers stationed in South Korea have somewhat declined since the end of the Cold War, the US remains theoretically committed to the defence of the ROK. As the US landings near Inchon were a decisive factor in the collapse of the Korean People's Army during the Korean War, preventing the US from ever deploying significant forces onto land is of high importance to the DPRK. While the destruction of ports and air bases by North Korean missile strikes might temporarily delay or complicate US reinforcements from reaching the Korean Peninsula, the amphibious capabilities of the US enable it to carry out landings without the need for harbours, thus doing little to prevent the US from landing its forces on the Korean Peninsula. In the immediate wake of the USA's pullback from Vietnam, North Korea is believed to have taken into consideration the US public opinion during a potential invasion of South Korea.[4] As significant casualties to US personnel were then a contributory factor in turning the US public against the war, ultimately leading the US to effectively abandon its ally South Vietnam, the North figured inflicting enough casualties could be sufficient to prompt a similar response in Korea. While such an abandonment was unthinkable for much of the post-Cold War period, US public opinion is difficult to predict in its new era of isolationism, and US high-level decision-making even more so. Another strategy the DPRK has continued to employ since the Cold War is to attempt to foster anti-US sentiment in the South using propaganda. Were this to be more effective, it might have led to a political climate sufficiently unfavourable to the deployment of US forces that it could ultimately have resulted in the disbandment of the entire USFK. Instead, USFK's end is more likely to come about from fissures in the ROK-US alliance, and most notably South Korean debate on its continued existence following US president Donald Trump's demands that it begin sharing the costs of the deployments. Last but not least, the DPRK, should it come into control of the whole of the Korean Peninsula, could attempt to hold its gains hostage with the threat of using WMDs against the region should any counter-invasion be mounted.

Whether or not its efforts at staving off a counter-attack by the ROK's allies would be successful or not, it is certain that speed would be of the essence if North invades South. One aspect of much importance in allowing such a lightning attack is logistics. When its supply lines faltered under the weight of the UN coalition's relentless aerial bombardment campaign, the North Korean attack finally ran out of steam at the Pusan Perimeter. Building upon this valuable experience, the DPRK has made stockpiling war material a top priority for its armed forces. Although under the guise of its Songun policies it had invested liberally in its stockpiles since long ago, the current sanctions regime complicates the KPA's ability to maintain them. Especially its oil reserves, essential for waging any kind of protracted war, have increasingly become hard to get by after China began to enforce economic sanctions more universally in 2017. The DPRK has since resorted to ship-to-ship transfers of coal and oil on the open ocean, a tactic which is unlikely to satisfy all its needs and which has not gone unnoticed by foreign observers. To increase the survivability of its stockpiles an elaborate network of underground storages has been constructed, which is constantly being renovated and expanded. In addition, virtually all of its industry of importance to the war effort (and a lot of its industry that is not as well) has since the 1960s been built underground, providing a challenge for those attempting to paralyse its production capacity. Aside from the roughly 300 factories already dedicated to producing arms and munitions, in wartime numerous factories ordinarily producing civilian commodities would be rerolled for military purposes. These measures combined with the fact that much of its industry is protected by dedicated AA sites means that the DPRK's wartime industry would be extraordinarily difficult to destroy. Overall stockpiles are believed to be sufficient to last for between one and three months of continuous fighting, meaning the success of an invasion would more than likely be decided within this period of time.[5] Beyond that, a lack of fuel especially would cripple not only the KPA's warfighting capacity but even its ability to move troops and supplies to the front, thus grinding the entire invasion to a halt. The North Korean leadership acknowledges this fact, and refers to its plans for a lightning attack as the 'One Blow Non-Stop Attack'. Similarly, in 1992 Kim Jong Il devised a strategy known as 'Occupying South Korea, All the Way to Pusan in Three Days'. Although the goal stated in its title is obviously a fantasy, in the 1990s it was believed by the leadership that occupying all of South Korea could be achieved within roughly a month.[6]

Perhaps the most important aspect in determining the outcome of a North Korean invasion attempt is the element of surprise. Even though the KPA's threat is often attributed to its large personnel numbers, it is the South that has a larger population pool to draw from. As such, it too maintains a large standing army and even larger reserves, which require anything from several days to weeks

A mobile field hospital pictured at a North Korean military exhibition. The DPRK, operating an army of disproportional size compared to its low GDP, is unlikely to be able to provide even basic medical services to the millions of military casualties that might be expected during wartime. (KCBC)

to mobilise.[7] In an extended prelude to a war with the DPRK, these forces could be mobilised in advance; what is more, the ROK's allies could put together a coalition and thus provide massive amounts of soldiers, potentially overwhelming anything the KPA can bring to bear. Therefore, should the North initiate hostilities, the attack will likely commence with as little warning as possible. Although a large force can already be mustered in under 48 hours, using a variety of deception tactics could allow the KPA more time to mobilise and as such maximise its chances in the conflict. Such tactics were for instance employed to great success during the 1973 Yom Kippur War, during which Egypt managed to mobilise much of its forces for a surprise attack on Israel and in doing so achieved impressive initial gains. Nowadays such a strategy will be much more difficult to pull off however due to advancements in surveillance technology, extremely pervasive signal intelligence (SIGINT) operations undertaken by the USA and not in the least because of the continuously high tensions on the Korean Peninsula. The ROK and its allies will as such likely be able to detect preparations for a long conflict, ranging from increased military activity, transport, mass mobilisation of civilians, workers and reserve forces and the shift to wartime production in factories.[8] Although the North can and presumably would forward deploy its forces under the guise of military exercises, this would lead to increased readiness or even mobilisation in the South, offsetting much of the advantage gained through such a tactic.

Once full mobilisation has begun however, the fact that war has broken out will be evident quickly enough by the commencement of massive artillery barrages targeting defensive positions south of the DMZ and various longer-ranged (ballistic) missile strikes at military bases, communications and logistics centres and any targets of high value both in South Korea and Japan, and possibly even Guam. North Korean electronic warfare units will attempt to disrupt communications and disable the Global Positioning System (GPS) required for many navigational systems and guidance modes in weaponry by jamming. Those operatives already stationed in the South and whatever forces can be quickly inserted by air, sea or even underground will aim to create as much chaos as possible, destroying important military facilities, assassinating high-ranking officials and drawing troops away that would otherwise be tasked with defending the DMZ. Although many of these tactics could be individually tackled in time, their combination would ensure an overwhelmingly destructive effect that could thoroughly disrupt operational or tactical decision making by the ROKA and USFK.[9] Following the massive artillery barrages targeting defences south of the DMZ, light infantry units and engineering vehicles will secure a safe passage through the massive minefields straddling the border and potentially finish the last metres of tunnels dug under the DMZ, allowing the infantry corps to pass. These infantry corps will then probe ROK defences, concentrating firepower on lesser defended corridors in order to create a gap that can be exploited by the Armoured Division, Mechanised Corps and Mechanised Infantry Divisions. Assaults are expected to occur through three main avenues of approach, with several smaller corridors allowing manoeuvres between them.[10] When particularly stiff resistance is encountered at any particular battlefield, the corridors allow KPAGF units to redirect their focus on weak spots where opposing forces are more easily overwhelmed. Once the front is breached through such corridors the remaining pockets of resistance should become isolated and subsequently dealt with with more ease. The Seoul Capital Area has grown to be one of the largest metropolitan areas in the world today, containing approximately half of South Korea's entire population. As such, it would be far too large to occupy should an invasion advance to this point, and the KPA's next course of action would likely be to isolate it and use its armoured/mechanised forces to bypass the city and continue the attack towards Pusan. The conquest of Seoul could then possibly be truly initiated by a second offensive of forces that took longer to mobilise; if the invasion is then thwarted farther down the peninsula retaking Seoul from such a force would become an immensely costly objective. Aside from the main thrust into South Korea responsible for destroying the bulk of ROKA forces above Seoul, it is likely a secondary army group would direct its offensive along the eastern side of the peninsula. Its task would be to secure

M-1991 SPGs during the 70th anniversary of the foundation of the Korean People's Army parade in February 2018. Note the AGLs and MANPADS mounted to the turret. (KCBC)

the eastern coastline and to execute flanking attacks in support of the primary thrust whenever necessary.

During all of these manoeuvres the KPA will have to maintain its momentum in order to deny opposing forces the opportunity to regroup and set up defensive lines. For this purpose the DPRK employs the so-called Strike Force concept, wherein a single unit is continually reinforced with additional units as its combat situation and needs evolve.[11] This allows it to bring much more firepower towards the battlefield, and more dynamically engage whatever threat it may encounter. Although several types of North Korean artillery exist that can support advancing KPAGF units from behind the DMZ in the initial phases of a war, such a unit may, for instance, see self-propelled artillery assigned to it as required. The existence of, for instance, self-propelled guns (SPGs) mounting automatic grenade launchers (AGLs) and man-portable air-defence systems (MANPADS) attest that such hybrid Strike Force units are expected to use their own artillery assets close to the front, as SPGs operating behind stable front lines would not require built-in air defence or anti-infantry assets.

Although these highly ambitious plans take into account feasibility and the KPA's weaknesses, a variety of factors cause them to have little chance of succeeding even in the crucial early phases of a war. Indeed, the successful creation of a second front will fully rely on the capacity to bring in troops by sea and air (in addition to those troops already clandestinely present), a feat which will be difficult to pull off and carries with it large risks. Additionally, its conventional forces will be hard pressed to execute the speedy advances required while navigating first the vast minefields and defensive structures near the DMZ, and then the highly urbanised, generally mountainous and river-veined landscape that lies beyond it. Meanwhile, once the initial shock from the strikes at air bases in the region has subsided, the DPRK is liable to swiftly lose the aerial battle for the peninsula so that the ROK and its allies would be free to carry out bombing sorties on advancing KPA columns. During the Korean War some of this disadvantage was mitigated by using the cover of night for operations, but nowadays the disparity in quality between night vision equipment of both sides (with much of the KPAAF not being qualified for night sorties, and the KPAGF traditionally relying mainly on older infrared searchlights for its AFVs) means that the KPA might be in an even worse position. Even though the distance between the DMZ and Seoul measures just some 40 kilometres, the South's defensive strategy is based around neutralising an invasion force before it has reached the city. Since losing the Seoul area would likely have a devastating effect both on operations and ROKA morale, South Korea presumably aims to decide much of the war's eventual course in the narrow strip of land that separates its capital from the DPRK's territory. Even should fate rule in the KPA's favour and it manages to complete its plans to the full, occupying the entire peninsula before substantial reinforcements can arrive, the war is not yet won. Beyond this point, the DPRK would have to devise a strategy to deter any forces from landing on its newly gained territory, or else it will surely be defeated in the long run.

Of course, this is not the only scenario for a full resumption of hostilities on the Korean Peninsula. While in the past this might have seemed implausible, nowadays an attempt to forcibly end the Kim regime's rule by a foreign power is all but unthinkable. Interestingly, part of the KPA's offensive-oriented structure also applies to a defensive scenario during wartime, as part of its defensive doctrine includes conducting massive counterattacks to repel forces from DPRK territory.[12] Actual defensive strategies are only employed in preparation of further offensive operations, and any breaches in KPA defensive lines are likely to be met with immediate counter-attacks to disrupt the opposing force's offensive.[13] Nonetheless, the North is absolutely riddled with defensive structures from the DMZ to its northernmost borders that could be used to complicate an invasion of its lands. Its two long coastlines, an unfortunate consequence of controlling the northern half of a peninsula, are defended by coastal defence systems, coastal artillery and vast fortifications nearly along their full length. The immediate area beyond the DMZ is set up so that any infrastructure that may benefit an invading power can be swiftly dismantled, to the point of having the option of releasing dam waters to flood areas further down south. Its vast network of AAA sites, underground bases and factories, and other pre-built fortifications could in wartime be manned by its massive reserve forces, and become difficult and very time consuming to destroy. Large scale efforts to better conceal its military factories and equipment also contribute towards hardening North Korea against any invasion, and electronic warfare (such as GPS jamming) and decoys would surely be employed in an attempt to reduce the efficacy of aerial sorties. Even after the 91 Capital Defence Corps has been defeated and the capital has been taken, the North Korean leadership likely aims to continue the fight from facilities in its highly wooded and mountainous north, and by encouraging guerilla activities in occupied territories. Of course, for the conflict to reach a point such as this it requires a level of restraint in using nuclear weapons that will likely not be present.

4
INFANTRY

Whether on the offensive or defensive, the individual prestations of a KPA soldier are supposed to ensure the KPA has an edge over any potential adversary it might find itself at odds with. Faced with opponents that could potentially outnumber the North during wartime, the KPA has put heavy emphasis on the performance of the individual soldier with slogans such as 'A revolutionary army should defeat the enemy's numerical and technical superiority with a political and ideological, strategic and tactical superiority!'. Thus, what the North lacks in numbers, it hopes to make up for by superior tactics and the determination of its soldiers. Nowadays this not only applies to the number of soldiers the North can muster, but also to the generally inferior equipment of a KPA soldier versus that of his Southern and US counterparts. This discrepancy is mainly the result of technological advances and new tactical requirements for the ROKA and US Army in equipping its soldiers. For one US soldier alone the costs of modern equipment and increasing amounts of additional gear (such as body armour, night vision equipment, radios and small UAVs) are close to $20,000 US.[1] The DPRK, operating an army of disproportionate size compared to its low GDP, is unable to follow this trend, and such equipment mostly remains reserved for its special operations forces.

Nonetheless, despite coping with a crumbling economy tormenting all modernisation projects of the KPA, the DPRK has steadily continued the modernisation and introduction of new hardware for its soldiers, albeit to a more limited scale than seen in other nations. This accomplishment is in no small part due to North Korea's large infantry weapons industry, which is completely self-sufficient in the production of anything from firearms to MANPADS and compared to other armament industries of North Korea is able to design, prototype and mass-produce such weaponry on a considerably faster and larger scale. While the small arms industry has its foundations in copying various foreign designs such as Soviet AK-pattern rifles and RPGs but also more advanced weaponry such as ATGMs and MANPADS, North Korea has since extensively modified these original designs while at the same time introducing a range of completely novel ones. This unique blend results in the highly exotic inventory of small arms and infantry equipment seen in today's Korean People's Army.

Compared to the founding of other armament industries the establishment of a small arms industry started off early in the DPRK. This entailed the production of Soviet PPSh-41 submachine guns (SMGs), a feat often circulated in North Korean propaganda even today. Produced as the Type-49 (referring to the year the weapon was first (mass-)produced), the Type-49 incorporated minor modifications over the original design by introducing a different shaped buttstock and a unique straight stick magazine (although most production Type-49s would make use of the original Soviet style 35-round box and 71-round drum magazines).[2] Produced in significant numbers, these guns supplemented copious amounts of Soviet and Chinese supplied Mosin-Nagants, PPS, DP-27s, Maxims and other weaponry dating from the Second World War. The KPA would also obtain significant numbers of US M3 SMGs and their Chinese copies from China, which were observed with the Red Youth Guard as recently as 2013. Most of the aforementioned Soviet weaponry remains in service with the Worker-Peasant Red Guard as well, providing the DPRK with a seemingly endless supply of small arms, albeit ostensibly hampered by nightmarish logistical

Kim Il Sung test-fires an indigenously produced Type-49 SMG on 12 December 1948 in front of several Soviet advisors and North Korean military personnel. (KCBC)

requirements. Standardisation in Worker-Peasant Red Guard units is practically unheard of. The large numbers of Soviet Second World War-era equipment fielded during the Korean War meant that the KPA faced the same problems as Soviet soldiers did during the Second World War, such as a lack of portable anti-tank weaponry. Relying on small numbers of unwieldy PTRS-41 anti-tank rifles and anti-tank grenades, the lack of modern anti-tank weaponry on the side of the communists resulted in peculiar situations where soldiers would climb onto tanks in an effort to find a way to disable them.

Overall, the average North Korean soldier following the armistice in 1953 was largely equipped and trained according to the doctrine of the Soviet and Chinese armies. For the North Koreans, this meant individual soldiers were typically lightly equipped and for a long time lacking in various basic resources. As this situation slowly began to change in Soviet-aligned countries, so it did in North Korea, with more modern weaponry dating from after the Second World War becoming increasingly prevalent over time. Initially taking delivery of anything the Soviet Union was willing to supply, it was during the 1960s when the DPRK became increasingly focused on developing and producing infantry weaponry indigenously. This strictly entailed

Worker-Peasant Red Guards raise their weapons as they set out on a field training exercise. The plethora of small arms visible in this image comprise Mosin-Nagants, Type-49s, AK-47s, DP-27s, TT-33s and RPG-2s: a logistical nightmare. (KCBC)

Worker-Peasant Red Guards aim their Type-58 assault rifles with bayonets fixed. The production of large quantities of more modern assault rifles for service with the KPAGF has meant that most Type-58s have now been relegated to the reserve forces. (KCBC)

the copying of small arms patterned after Soviet designs however, and it would take several more decades before the equipment of the average KPA soldier became distinctly North Korean.

During this period North Korea began producing the ubiquitous AK-47 under the designation of Type-58. The Kalashnikov rifle, a symbol of communism and struggle against colonialism, was put into production by many countries, and North Korea was no exception. While initial production examples of the Type-58 appear to have been assembled from parts delivered by the Soviets, North Korean parts quickly began replacing the Soviet ones, heralding the start of true indigenous production. This however meant that the North Koreans ran into the same problems that had troubled the Soviets: it was difficult and expensive to mass-produce the weapon's milled receiver. As a result, the number of Type-58s produced is believed to have been limited, at least when compared to later types of assault rifles produced by the DPRK. The Soviets eventually solved this problem by redesigning the rifle with a stamped receiver, becoming the AKM, which entered service with the Soviet Army in 1959. North Korea followed suit nine years later, first attempting to assuage demand for a new rifle by copying the Soviet SKS carbine as the Type-63 before importing and later producing an indigenous copy of the AKM under the designation of Type-68. The Type-68 features several differences over the original AKM, most notably forgoing the AKM's typical muzzle compensator and rate reducer. A lighter folding-stock version featuring holes for weight reduction was also fielded alongside the fixed stock version. Still in service with the Korean People's Army but mostly with the Worker-Peasant Red Guard, the Type-68 and Type-58 are commonly seen with 20-round magazines instead of the ordinary 30-round magazines. A feature

North Korea is one of several nations that continue to use rifle grenades. These rifle grenades fitted on Type-68s are based on the Polish PGN-60 anti-tank projectile. (NK Pro)

These parading North Korean soldiers wield Type-68s outfitted with dummy rifle grenades based on the Polish KGN fragmentation projectile. Also notice the 20 round magazines, which are noticeably smaller than the 30 round magazines seen in the previous image. Although originally intended for use with tankers, the 20 round magazines found their way to many regular KPAGF units as well. (NK Pro)

that is also reserved for Type-58/68 assault rifles is the capability to fire at least two types of rifle grenades based on the Polish PGN-60 anti-tank and KGN fragmentation projectiles. Although nowadays unlikely to penetrate the armour of modern tanks, these projectiles do much to increase the firepower of reserve forces against light armour and other soft targets.

Type-58 and Type-68 rifles were widely exported to friendly nations around the world, including to Peru, where the latter are reportedly known as AK-Corea, which purchased 100,000 rifles for a price 80 percent lower than the next closest bid. Another reported delivery was for 100,000 rifles to Cuba along with millions of rounds of ammunition free of charge, supposedly after the Soviet Union refused the same Cuban order. North Korea would also help set up a production line for Ethiopia in the late 1980s, tailored to production of the Type-68.[3] Similarly, Syria is believed to have been enabled the production of small numbers of Type-68s in the late 1980s and early 1990s.[4] Projects of a comparable nature set up in Somalia and Tanzania in the 1980s do not appear to have been successful however.[5] Other users of the Type-68 include countries like the DR Congo, Mozambique, Nicaragua (following Cuban deliveries), Yemen and Zambia. At the home front, the mass production of Type-58s and Type-68s gave North Korean soldiers a distinct advantage over South Korean soldiers, which were still equipped with the M1 Garand and M2 Carbines until M16s began to be introduced in the 1970s.

North Korea also managed to offset the lack of anti-tank weaponry it was previously plagued with during the Korean War by acquiring and later producing large quantities of rifle anti-tank grenades, anti-tank mines, recoilless rifles (RCLs) and RPG-2 shoulder-fired anti-tank weapons. The RPG-2, which appears to have enjoyed a short indigenous production run in the late 1950s, would later be supplemented by even larger numbers of domestically-produced RPG-7s known as the Type-68 in the DPRK, which relegated the RPG-2 to reserve forces which still use them in large numbers today. In addition to producing the launcher itself, the DPRK also produces several types of rocket-propelled grenades for the Type-68, including a domestic copy of the standard PG-7 round known as the F-7, and a PG-7M lookalike that is reportedly usable out to slightly greater ranges. These rounds and their associated launchers have shown up throughout the world, including in Syria, Libya, Mali, Myanmar, Gaza and Egypt, which seized 30,000 rounds in 2017 after a tip-off by the United States intelligence services that a North Korean freighter nearing the Suez Canal could be carrying illicit cargo, the largest seizure of DPRK weaponry ever to have occurred since the implementation of sanctions.[6] In a surprising turn of events, the destination of the ship was revealed to be the country that seized the illicit cargo: Egypt. This shows that despite international sanctions forbidding countries from purchasing North Korean weaponry, those very same weapons remain popular merchandise around the world, even to some of the nations ostensibly adhering to the sanctions regime. In this particular case, the Egyptians were ill-advised in their purchase not only due to the illegal nature of the deal. Despite bearing markings that declared the munitions had been produced as late as March 2016, they were in fact of much older stock.[7]

Extensive efforts would be put into the design and production of general-purpose machine guns (GPMGs), for which North Korea utilised the Soviet 7.62x54mmR PK design as a basis, which itself entered service only in very meagre numbers. Its indigenous designs would supplement older types of GPMGs such as the Soviet RP-46, a development of the DP-27, and its North Korean Type-64 copy, which are now mainly relegated to reserve forces. Its first and rarest production example was designated the Type-68 (although it is sometimes erroneously identified as the Type-82 – which would imply it was a much more mature design), which left most of the critical design aspects of the PK unaltered including the barrel fluting that was omitted on later PK variants. Most notable is the addition of a large square tangent sight for long distance fire, and a stock that in contrast to the original one is characteristically un-hollowed. Although these guns are nowadays rare even in North Korean service due to their relatively short production run, a single example found in Zimbabwe attests to the fact that at least some were exported as well.[8] Production soon shifted to the Type-73, which despite still sharing many design components with the Type-68 and PK, may be one of the most peculiar GPMGs ever mass-produced. Patterned after the Czechoslovakian vz. 52 LMG which used the lighter 7.62x45mm and 7.62x39mm cartridges, it has two separate feeds allowing it to be either belt-fed or magazine-fed from a 30-round top-mounted curved box magazine. A new tangent sight and barrel attachment were developed in order to be able to see past the magazine, although much of the view remains obscured even when the box magazine is not fitted due to the awkward feed cover. While it is seldomly seen used, the muzzle brake and part of the barrel can be screwed off to unveil a different barrel attachment (the barrel end can be locked into place under the gun when it is not being used), which has the unique function of firing rifle grenades – an unprecedented feature for GPMGs. These modifications serve to greatly increase the versatility of the Type-73, allowing it to execute firing missions typically reserved for machine guns in different classes. Nevertheless, actual combat efficacy is hampered by increased complexity and bulkiness, and combined with the fact that it lacks a convenient 100-round magazine like that of the PK, thus requiring a dedicated loader in the fire support role, the overall increases in its scope of operations seem hardly worthwhile. Large numbers of Type-73s were exported to Iran, which used them extensively in the Iran-Iraq War and is responsible for the proliferation of the weapon to such nations as Iraq, Syria and Yemen. Small numbers still in use with Ugandan police attest to previously undocumented deliveries to that country as well. In late 2024, substantial numbers of Type-73s were also exported to Russia for use in the Russo-Ukrainian War, where their excessive

Soldiers prepare to fire their Type-73s GPMGs during a firing contest. (KCBC)

A Type-73 GPMG mounted on a motorcycle sidecar, along with its Russian operators, in early 2025 during the Russo-Ukrainian War. (Milinfolive)

A look at a rare Type-68 GPMG recovered from an infiltration craft that sank during the Battle of Amami-Ōshima in 2001. (Tarao)

weight of over 10kg made them ill-favoured with Russian soldiers that got an opportunity to use them.

While the KPA has yet to introduce a more modern type of GPMG replacing the versatile but cumbersome Type-73, there have been attempts at developing other types of 7.62x54mmR machineguns. One particularly unique example of this is a six-barrelled rotary machine gun which closely mimics the exterior of the US M134 Minigun and was likely developed for export in the early 1990s. It was demonstrated to buyers from Sri Lanka and included in armament procurement negotiations with Syria in September 2016, but does not appear to have entered active service with the KPA itself, despite the proliferation of different calibre rotary weapons since the 1990s.[9] [10] Its development serves as an important reminder of the impressive drive behind North Korea's indigenous armament industry however, and the fact that this weapon is largely unknown to analysts to this day shows that surprises in its small arms inventory must be reckoned with.

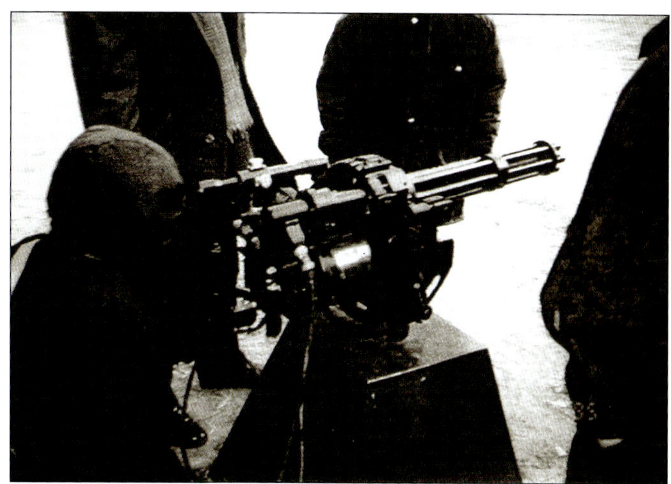

The 'Gun 2' 7.62x54mmR rotary machine gun showcased in North Korea to buyers from Sri Lanka. (Authors' archive)

In service alongside the Type-68 and Type-73 GPMGs are large numbers of squad automatic weapons, the most ubiquitous of which is the 7.62x39mm RPD, produced in the DPRK as the Type-62, which uses a 100-round drum magazine. Large scale production of an indigenous variant of the 5.45×39mm RPK-74 has meanwhile meant that most RPDs have been relegated for use with the reserve forces, likely only remaining in service with KPAGF units still using the 7.62x39mm Type-68 assault rifle as their primary service weapon. In contrast with the original Soviet design, later North Korean copies of the RPK-74 would forgo the Soviet fixed stock for side-folding or top-folding stocks, increasing the compactness and versatility of the weapon. The RPK-74 copy has in recent times been spotted with a new high-capacity casket magazine that is notably fatter than the one ordinarily used, and likely holds double the rounds for an impressive total of 90 rounds. Recent experimentation with different types of modern high-capacity magazines have shown a preference for greater ammunition loads, but the increased complexity and weight associated with these designs does result in slightly reduced performance.

North Korea decided to take a whole different path for the production of handguns, relying on both Western and Soviet designs to provide the KPA with a highly diverse inventory. This design craze might have been partially motivated by Kim Jong Il's fondness of small arms, who is often depicted in propaganda footage wielding different types of handguns in the 1980s and 1990s. Unsurprisingly, only a limited number of designs would eventually enter service,

North Korean soldiers during the 105th anniversary of Kim Il Sung's birthday parade of 2017 wielding RPK-74-derived squad automatic weapons with side-folding stocks and high-capacity casket magazines. (NK Pro)

with eccentric designs such as an apparent underwater bolt revolver perhaps best left to the drawing board. The most prolific users of handguns have generally been infiltrators and spies belonging to North Korea's foreign intelligence apparatus, which mainly utilised various foreign types along with a number of North Korean designs also serving with the KPA. Most foreign types in use are of Western origin and are sometimes equipped with suppressors for stealthy operations. Many of the examples known to be in use were found in the aftermath of such missions which went awry, and handguns not used by special forces are therefore much less known. One of the oldest types produced in the DPRK is also one of the oddest. First mass-produced in 1964, this indigenous variant of the Belgian FN M1900 was produced some 64 years after its inception in 1900. While the Type-64 was basically an antique by the time it was commissioned, it appears that the FN M1900 was at least in part chosen for its symbolic worth: it was this weapon that was used by An Jung Geun to assassinate the Japanese Resident-General of Korea Itō Hirobumi during the Japanese occupation of Korea, an event that is still remembered in both North and South Korea.[11] Not all of its workings were copied outright however, and instead of the original .32 ACP round it uses the highly similar 7.62x17mm Type-64 ammunition which was developed for China's own Type-64 handgun years before. While it would be succeeded by more modern designs, modified suppressor-equipped variants of the Type-64 were found on the bodies of North Korea infiltrators decades after its initial production. Another handgun, known variously as the Type-68 and Type-70 but only marked with 조선 7.62 (Chosun 7.62) uses the same anomalous round and stems from the same time period, but appears to have been loosely based on the Soviet Makarov and a variety of other designs. The necessity to mark these two handguns with their calibre likely arose due to the fact that the Czechoslovakian Škorpion vz. 61 had also just entered service, which does use the .32 ACP cartridge. The trend of copying foreign small arms but adapting their inner workings to North Korean requirements was continued in the Type-66, a firearm closely resembling the Browning Hi-Power but which was actually based on and chambered for the cartridge of the Soviet TT-33 Tokarev pistol. Although this handgun seems to have entered service in greater numbers, the spate of new designs continued until the North ultimately produced a copy of the highly popular Czechoslovak CZ 75 in the late 1980s, designated as Paektusan (referring to Mount Paektu). This gun remains the primary service pistol of the KPA to this day, with a reworked variant utilising extended-capacity magazines recently having entered service.

With the production of several types of assault rifles, GPMGs and handguns well underway, North Korea however still lagged behind in the introduction of designated marksman rifles and sniper rifles into its ranks. While North Korea had an ample supply of Mosin-Nagant bolt-action rifles and PTRS and PTRD anti-tank rifles (which can be used in the anti-materiel rifle role) left over from the Korean War, few if any of these appear to have been utilised as long-range high-precision rifles. This contrasts with Soviet strategic thinking, in which designated marksman rifles are widely used as a squad support weapon. It was not until the late 1970s that North Korea adopted its own designated marksman rifle. Often claimed to be a direct copy of the Yugoslav Zastava M76, this rifle is actually of an indigenous design largely derived from the Romanian PSL, thus also using the standard 7.62x54mmR instead of the M76's 7.92x57mm Mauser. The link with Romania is also apparent in its optics, which are a direct copy of the Romanian LPS 4×6° TIP2 telescopic sight and a night sight reminiscent of the 1PN58 (designated as Sniper Scope-78 and Night Scope-78 respectively). Several other designated marksman

A suppressor-equipped FN Baby Browning that was found on the body of a North Korean infiltrator after a 1980 seaborne infiltration attempt went awry. The small size of this handgun even with a suppressor attached made it a popular choice for North Korean infiltrators. Three captured Škorpion vz. 61s can be seen in the background. (Korean Television (KTV))

The latest variant Paektusan pistol. Note the faint 'Paektusan' print in front of the safety and Kim Jong Il's autograph on the grip. (KCBC)

rifles and sniper rifles mostly based on hunting rifles have been spotted over the years, but none appear to have entered service with the KPA in any significant numbers. More serious developments first spotted during the Self-Defence-2021 exhibition in October 2021 constitute a sniper rifle (possibly chambered in 7.62×54mmR) of similar appearance to the renowned Accuracy International Arctic Warfare rifle, and an anti-materiel rifle reminiscent of the Russian KVSK possibly chambered in 12.7×108mm. Though neither has yet been seen in use with regular units, it may be presumed North Korea intends to produce them for this purpose in the future. In 2023, Kim Jong Un examined yet another new sniper rifle closely resembling the Russian DVL-10 M2. In a follow-up visit to the same small arms factory the next year, a variant with a sizeable integrated suppressor was showcased, which was later claimed to be '7.62mm' in calibre (likely referring to .308 Winchester).[12] Both types utilise different optics, and a front-mountable thermal device seems to be available as well. In an interview with the Russian newspaper *Mash*, Vladislav Lobaev claimed that shortly prior to early 2022 several Koreans came to his company to purchase three DVL-10 M1 rifles for hunting purposes, suggesting that the North Korean examples are unlicensed copies.[13] The unveiling of multiple types of sniper rifles suggests that North Korea is still testing various models before considering their widespread adoption within the KPAGF and SOF. The fluidity of the situation was emphasised further during SOF exercises in April 2025, which saw Kim Jong Un wielding yet another new sniper rifle claimed to be newly developed and intended for

On exhibit at the Self-Defence-2021 exhibition were a sniper rifle reminiscent of the Accuracy International Arctic Warfare rifle and an anti-materiel rifle. Neither of these weapons have yet been observed in active military use. (KCBC)

SOF units. Curiously, in this instance it appeared to have been an extremely faithful copy of the Steyr SSG 08, illustrating a growing North Korean adeptness in reverse engineering foreign firearms.

Although a historic lack of dedicated assets for long-range shooting is perhaps surprising, KPA doctrine appears to have heavily favoured close quarters infantry combat over longer-range engagements, where many of the KPA's deficiencies quickly come into play. Bayonets can be fitted to most assault rifles in use with the DPRK and are frequently featured in propaganda footage and parades. Combat sports have also been part of KPA and particularly special operations forces training, which according to one North Korean defector enabled them to fight 10 men without guns.[14] The most notable of these is Kyoksul, a well-rounded combat sport that is highly suitable for military forces due to its diverse attributes. Apparently impressed with the combat sport, the KPA was requested by several Warsaw Pact nations in the 1980s to show off Kyoksul, with

This sniper rifle, reminiscent of the Russian DVL-10 M2, is among several new designs revealed in recent years. Note the poster, which displays a new AK-pattern assault rifle based on the AK-12/19, optionally chambered in both 5.45x39mm and 5.56x45mm NATO. (KCBC)

Hungary and Poland later adopting the sport for its own military and East Germany incorporating suitable elements into its own close disciplines.[15] Kyoksul is also practised in Cuba, and Korean instructors have been active in nations such as Libya, training elite units in the martial arts and use of small arms.[16]

One of the greatest revolutions in the KPA's infantry weapons inventory entailed the introduction and production of MANPADS and ATGMs, which commenced with deliveries of the 9K32 Strela-2 MANPADS and 9M14 Malyutka ATGMs. These were supposedly sourced from Egypt in 1974 after which North Korea set out to reverse engineer them by the late 1970s, but other sources simply mention the Soviet Union aiding in setting up industries for such systems in the late 1970s.[17] Chinese HN-5A MANPADS and HJ-73 ATGMs (which are Chinese variants of the 9K32 and 9M14, respectively) are also reported to have been delivered in the mid 1970s or 1980s, but are difficult to distinguish from their Soviet predecessors.[18] Wherever the origin may lie, North Korean variants began to proliferate, with a copy of the 9M14 known as the Bulsae-1 (Phoenix-1) and various types of 9K32-derived MANPADS known as the CSA-3A, PGLM and other names.[19] The 9M14 in fact did not constitute the first ATGM in KPA service, with the older 3M6 Shmel based on the 2P26 light truck platform as well as the 2P27 BRDM-1-based ATGM carrier participating in the parade for the 40th anniversary of the Korean People's Revolutionary Army in April 1972. As this cumbersomely large system cannot be used by infantry and in fact represents one of the oldest manual command to line of sight (MCLOS) ATGM designs in existence it is unlikely to still be in use with the KPA today.[20]

Despite now being self-sufficient in the production of anything from handguns to MANPADS, the break with the Soviet Union meant that the DPRK was essentially cut off from more modern designs for a decade. While relations with China flourished during this period, the Chinese small arms industry could not offer anything more advanced than was already being produced by North Korea either. The DPRK continued producing several types of proven small arms, yet their efficacy was now seriously lagging behind those used by nations such as the USA and ROK. Although this was less of an issue for pistols or assault rifles, it posed a serious problem for systems like ATGMs and MANPADS, which are more reliant on technological advancements to keep up with increased armour protection and countermeasures. With a gradual rapprochement between North Korea and the Soviet Union in the mid 1980s, the DPRK sought to mend this technological backlog by acquiring and securing license contracts for the AK-74, the 9K111 Fagot ATGM system and the 9K34 Strela-3 and later 9K310 Igla-1 MANPADS, with 9K310s featuring prominently on a variety of fighting vehicles during the 1992 parade commemorating the 60th anniversary of the Korean People's Army. North Korea would spend the next decades producing ever improved variants of these designs, resulting in an inventory that is still in fact mostly based on this shipment, albeit greatly modernised and with a uniquely North Korean influence.

Having gradually lost the aerial advantage it previously enjoyed over the Republic of Korea Air Force (ROKAF) following the Korean War, and with the annihilation of North Korean troop concentrations and supply lines by US and UN airpower during the Korean War likely still fresh in memory, MANPADS were weapons systems the KPA was all too glad to invest in. Being relatively cheap to produce and easy to operate, the widespread deployment of MANPADS is an effective means of giving infantry a way to defend themselves from aerial threats within five kilometres and is certain to inflict significant losses on an opposing air force during wartime. North Korea is an extremely prolific user of these systems, mounting them on many of their vehicles and ships and also exporting them to various nations including Syria, Mozambique, Vietnam and possibly South Sudan.[21] [22] After first copying the 9K310 Igla-1 in the 1990s, access to the more advanced 9K38 Igla with 9M39 missile was likely purchased from Russia in the early 2000s, allowing for the production of a modernised variant known as the HT-16PGJ incorporating the 9M39 missile's seeker and aerodynamic advancements.[23] [24] This upgraded variant, which is sometimes marketed as the SA-16M after the NATO designation of the 9K310, also appears to have slightly reduced weight and extended maximum range of 6,000 metres, as well as a proximity fuse. Despite these changes, it reportedly maintains compatibility with the 9M313 and 9M39. It is possible that access to examples of the US FIM-92 Stinger also aided in its design, but its externalities still resemble that of the 9K310 the most.[25] A still newer variant more resembling the 9K38 Igla or 9K338 Igla-S was first showcased on vehicles during the 2010 parade for the 65th anniversary of the Workers' Party, but appears to have yet to enter widespread service.

Legacy Soviet designs seem to have mostly outlived their potential for improvements however, as in October 2021 at the Self-Defence-2021 exhibition alongside Igla derivatives a MANPADS design was showcased that is of entirely novel design. Both shorter and fatter, it should be more convenient to transport by infantry and special forces, as well as potentially pack a larger warhead and seeker so as to defeat sturdier aircraft with advanced countermeasures. Outside this display it has not yet been spotted however, suggesting the new MANPADS has yet to enter (mass-)production.

North Korea also faced an increased obsolescence of its ATGM arsenal by the mid 1980s, which became increasingly dire after the deployment of the US M1 Abrams MBT to South Korea as part of the USFK, as well as the development of the ROKA K1 MBT. Still relying on masses of outdated Bulsae-1s and the even more ancient 3M6 Shmel, both notoriously difficult to steer and suffering from poor armour penetration characteristics against more modern tanks, a newer type of ATGM was desperately needed. In the 1980s, North Korea began to acquire and possibly manufacture large numbers of Soviet 9K111 Fagot missile systems with the 9M111-2 missile. Still a relatively modern system in the late 1980s, it represented a modest improvement over the Bulsae-1 in terms of armour penetration, and a steep one in terms of handling.[26] Perhaps more importantly, it gave the DPRK a design to improve on – something it would do in the

A Turkmen rebel shows off a North Korean HT-16PGJ MANPADS in Latakia, Syria in mid 2015. (Authors' archive)

The widespread deployment of MANPADS in the KPA means that several types are often operated alongside each other. Three different MANPADS can be seen in this image (first three MANPADS from left to right): the Igla-1, the North Korean HT-16PGJ and an Igla-1 using a modernised missile. (KCBC)

decades that followed. Most notably, it would soon introduce a new variant – possibly aided in development by the transfer one or more BGM-71 TOW missiles from Ethiopia in the 1990s – which uses a modified launcher and missile utilising laser beam-riding semi-automatic command to line of sight (SACLOS) guidance (i.e. semi-active laser homing (SALH)).[27] [28] By fitting a laser to the launcher and a sensor in the rear of the missile, the need for a wire to relay controls is negated, allowing the system to be more environmentally resistant (many wire-guided ATGMs cannot be fired over bodies of water) and more accurate. Since the laser can be quite narrow and extremely weak, the excellent countermeasure-resistant properties of wire-guided ATGMs are preserved. As a matter of fact, modernised and more compact variants of the launcher include what appears to be a separate anti-dazzling optic, included to expand countermeasure resistance to laser dazzling practices. Naming practices of this unique Fagot variant are, as often the case with North Korean armament, a little complicated. Although earlier variants, which aside from the guidance preserved other characteristics of the 9M111-2 such as the range, armour penetration and weight, received the designation Bulsae-2 (or AT-4, after the NATO designation of the 9K111, when exported), later variants would be called the Bulsae-4 and Bulsae-4M. Whether a Bulsae-3 also existed and represented another incremental improvement over the original 9K111 (or perhaps a prototype of the later Bulsae-5) is unknown, but it is known that the Bulsae-4 features both an improved range of up to 3,000 metres and improved armour penetration of 600–800mm (compared to 2,500 metres and 460mm for the 9M111-2).

A test of the Bulsae-4M, which currently constitutes North Korea's most advanced development in this line, was personally attended by Kim Jong Un in February 2016. During the testing, Kim Jong Un examined several launches of the man-portable system against at least two different targets, a concrete building and an indigenous Chonma-216 MBT, using two different warheads: a 'thermal pressure warhead' as well as a 'focusing warhead', with the former marked by a single red stripe and the latter three white stripes on the missile tube.[29] The use of a Chonma-216 tank (and possibly even two) as a target is highly remarkable, as this vehicle represented the DPRK's most modern MBT design up until 2009, possibly indicating that it was believed the ATGM should be tested against a properly armoured adversary. Still, it appears the shaped charge warhead was not the aspect that had been upgraded, with instead the range of the ATGM enhanced further to an impressive 4,000 metres without increasing the size of the system.

An unknown number of Bulsae-2s were exported to Iran in the 2000s, which smuggled them to the Izz ad-Din al-Qassam Brigades (the military wing of Hamas) in Gaza, where it was pitted against the Israeli Merkava Trophy active protection system to unknown success.[30] Another batch also ended up with the al-Nasser Salah al-Deen Brigades in Gaza.[31] Additionally, the Government of National Accord in Libya is thought to use the system, and Myanmar might have received the Bulsae-4, though in both cases it is unknown since when and in what numbers. Light vehicles, primarily simple trucks and jeeps, are known to mount these systems in KPA service, thus constituting light mobile ATGM platforms. A dedicated ATGM carrier based on the 323 APC chassis using the 9M14 ATGM was also being manufactured by the early 1980s, mounting five missiles in similar fashion to the Soviet 9P133 BRDM-2-based ATGM carrier in a retractable compartment on its rear. A 14.5mm KPV added to the front of the vehicle seriously risks obstructing the operator, and it appears other variants which lack this secondary armament also exist (possibly based on the Tokchon chassis).

The DPRK has also attempted to address the obsolescence of its ageing Bulsae-1 ATGMs as witnessed by a contract signed in late 2013 calling for the remodelling and modernisation of Malyutka ATGMs amongst the upgrading and delivery of a host of other weaponry by North Korea to Mozambique.[32] Although the contract provides no specific details on what the upgrade entails, it can be assumed the DPRK has spent considerable effort on upgrading its existing inventory of missiles or even producing newer variants in similar fashion to the upgrading of the Bulsae-2 to maintain the system's relevance in twenty-first century warfare. Such upgrades could include the fitting of a tandem high explosive anti-tank

(HEAT) warhead for increased armour penetration, a two-stage booster/sustain motor allowing for increased range or perhaps most likely, the replacement of the Malyutka's difficult to master MCLOS guidance in favour of SACLOS guidance.

Mere upgrades of these old Cold War relics are entirely insufficient to counter the advances in South Korea's armour forces however, and the 2010s have seen the introduction of two new modern ATGMs as a result. The first, under development at least since the start of the 2010s and known as the Bulsae-5, constitutes a direct copy of the potent Russian 9M133 Kornet.[33] Although it remains unknown whether North Korea sourced this technology directly from Russia or from another state or non-state actor, Syria is said to have provided eight missiles to North Korea in 2008, supposedly for research purposes.[34] Representing a leap in effectiveness over earlier available ATGMs, it is not unlikely that reverse engineering of the 9M133 immediately received high priority by the defence industry. First definitively showcased as part of a weapons package installed on the Songun-915 MBT during the parade for the 70th anniversary of the foundation of the Korean People's Army in February 2018, the deployment of these ATGMs on a variety of platforms as well as with dedicated tank-hunter teams could endanger even the most modern tank designs the ROK and US can bring to the field. They boast a range of 5,500 metres, and achieve well over 1,000mm RHA (rolled homogenous armour) penetration after defeating explosive reactive armour (ERA). While the copy appears to be largely faithful to the original, the 1PN79-1 thermal sight was omitted, meaning its night-fighting capabilities are severely diminished.

A soldier of the Izz ad-Din al-Qassam Brigades takes aim with his Bulsae-2 launcher somewhere in Gaza. (Izz ad-Din al-Qassam Brigades)

A North Korean soldier test-fires an upgraded Bulsae-2 ATGM in February 2016. (KCBC)

A penetrating hit of a Bulsae-2 ATGM causes the turret of a Chonma-216 MBT to be violently blown off, reminiscent of combat footage of tanks in Ukraine. The same target was reused in a 2024 test of loitering munitions. (KCBC)

A shorter-ranged and lighter anti-tank weapon of the recent past appears to have an altogether more surprising heritage. First showcased during the parade for the 90th anniversary of the Korean People's Revolutionary Army in April 2022, little is as yet known about this potentially significant new design. Disconcertingly, it appears to share a suspiciously large number of external features with the Israeli Spike-SR fire-and-forget anti-tank weapon, though there is no clear path for it to have made its way into North Korean hands. Lacking advanced optics, these types of disposable systems are typically used out to no further than 1,500 metres, and use target recognition software to guide itself after launched, so that no operator action is required after firing. Cost might limit the development and production of these new systems as well as the Bulsae-5 however, and they will likely continue to be supplemented by older designs.[35]

In the meantime, more conventional infantry weaponry also received its fair share of attention. In line with many Soviet-aligned nations of the day, North Korea began producing its own copy of the AK-74 under the designation of Type-88 in the late 1980s. Nowadays, the Type-88 has been produced in such large numbers that even parts of the Worker-Peasant Red Guard are equipped with these rifles, and it has replaced older AK-derivatives in many KPA units. Preferred due to the improved performance and lighter weight of the 5.45x39mm round over the 7.62x39mm, the significance of the rifle is evident in footage of Kim Il Sung inspecting Soviet-delivered AK(S)-74s in 1986, and of the leadership comparing AK-74s to other service rifles, including those of the ROKA, in years hence. As a cost-saving measure, North Korea initially produced a steel magazine instead of the AK-74's lighter 'Bakelite' magazine, albeit changed in shape and adapted to hold the smaller 5.45x39mm round.[36] While initial examples made use of a wooden stock patterned after the original Soviet design, later variants with a side-folding stock similar to the AKS-74 or a unique top-folding stock are more commonly seen, which is sometimes referred to as the Type-88-1 and Type-88-2 respectively. Type-88s are also sometimes spotted with Soviet 40mm GP-25 under-barrel grenade launchers, with their prevalence especially on more modern production Type-88s especially suggesting these are also manufactured indigenously. Despite its widespread introduction, the Type-88 failed to secure any substantial sales abroad, and Zambia is so far the only country confirmed to have operated a number of examples.

As production of the Type-88 continued, so did introductions of incremental refinements, and during the 2000s newer variants were

Women can serve in most areas of the KPA, like this designated marksman in a ghillie suit with a PSL-derived rifle. (Artwork by Adam Hook)

A North Korean soldier holding an embellished Type-73 GPMG. Engraved chromed variants such as these are usually gifted by the leadership to excelling servicemen during visits. (Artwork by Adam Hook)

A North Korean soldier wields a shortened Type-88 with top-folding stock and helical magazine, and the new stand-alone rocket launcher with top-folding stock slung around his neck. Note the colourful camouflage pattern, flak jacket and ceremonial gold-plated binoculars. (Artwork by Adam Hook)

Above: A Bulsae-5 launcher on a tractor-towed platform during the 73rd anniversary of the foundation of the DPRK in September 2021. (KCBC)

Right: Kim Jong Un inspects a soldier with a Spike-SR-inspired rocket launcher prior to the April 2022 parade. (KCBC)

adopted, providing the KPA with a rifle similar to the AK-74M in appearance. These rifles adopt the same polymer furniture of the AK-74M, although most production examples make use of the side- or top-folding stock, completely replacing the wooden components of the original Type-88. Produced alongside is a lighter plastic magazine, which now appears to be slowly finding its way into units operating older types of Type-88s as well. The new appearance of these Type-88s has led some to dub the rifle the Type-98, although this designation is not known to be in use in North Korea.

Perhaps the most distinctive variants of the Type-88 are those examples awarded personally to soldiers by the current leader, during visits to various military units throughout the country. These are chrome-plated and lavishly engraved arms, which come in a wide variety of types depending on the rank and accomplishments of the recipients, and even include an autographed plaque on the side. The general procedure of such visits often starts with Kim inspecting a certain military unit or exercise, after which the ceremony is started. Typically, but not always, three objects are handed out: a chrome-plated Type-88 rifle, a chrome-plated Type-73 GPMG and a pair of gold-plated binoculars. After this, all unit personnel line up – often on a stage set up specifically for this purpose – for a group picture with the Supreme Leader in the middle and the recipients of the

Kim Il Sung and Kim Jong Il inspecting two Soviet AK-74s and an AKS-74 in April 1986. Note the AGS-17 to the right. (KCBC)

new shiny weaponry close by his side. This tradition of 'gift politics' traces back to the Kim Il Sung era but was intensified by Kim Jong Il and subsequently continued by Kim Jong Un. What results is a peculiar situation where in exercises (and also likely extending to wartime use) well-camouflaged soldiers are easily visible by their shiny chrome-plated weaponry. A more reasonable adoption of chrome-plated weaponry has been for honour guards during official state events. However, these are often of a different type – such as the Type-58, Type-63 and the Type-68 –– and presumably issued to these personnel for aesthetic purposes.

Type-88-related developments accelerated in the 2010s, the first indication of which was the adoption of helical magazines for Type-88s in use with personal bodyguards of the Kim family as early as 2010. Using an innovative helical-shaped design, helical magazines are capable of holding extremely large numbers of rounds while remaining relatively lightweight and compact. Drawbacks that have prevented their more widespread use by other nations include the fact that they are quite complex and therefore expensive and more prone to malfunction. Additionally, using them on weaponry not designed with the use of helical magazines in mind potentially destabilises them due to their heavy weight. The North Korean variant is in fact the first such design to be deployed en masse, with large numbers showcased with regular units and SOF in recent parades, and also the first to utilise the concept for an assault rifle cartridge. Assuming a staggered packing of the cartridges, over 150 rounds can be held in a single magazine for a total weight of over two kilogrammes. Since

A lavishly engraved and chrome-plated Paektusan pistol. This example was part of a batch gifted to North Korean military officials and thus carries Kim Jong Un's autograph in gold lettering on the grip. (KCBC)

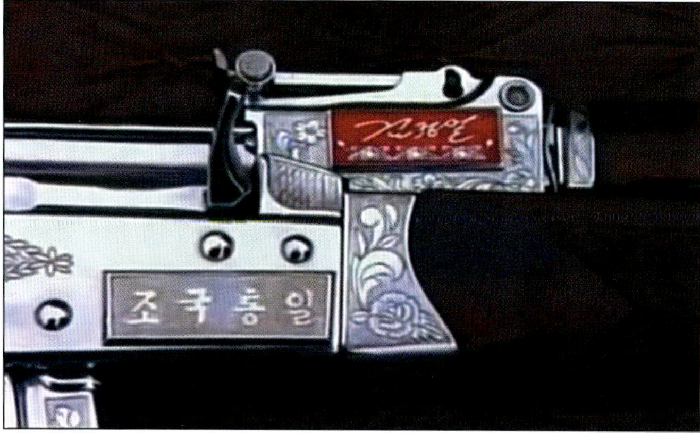

Detail of an engraved and chrome-plated Type-88. Note the engraving 'Reunification of the fatherland' on the side. (KCBC)

Reminiscent of the Russian PP-19 Bizon, the carbine version of the Type-88 is optimised for operations in the urban terrain that is ubiquitous in the South. This example is of the newer type equipped with a telescopic sight attached to the Picatinny-type rails, a flashlight and plastic furniture. (KCBC)

two spare magazines are typically carried, this means a minimum of 450 rounds are available if no regular magazines are carried alongside. A smaller helical magazine capable of holding at least 80 rounds is used on a different, carbine variant of the Type-88 that has entered service since the mid 2010s. First spotted during a SOF drill in December 2016 simulating a raid of South Korea's Blue House, this weapon features a significantly shortened gas tube, barrel and muzzle brake, which combined with its metal top-folding stock makes for a very compact weapon somewhat akin to the AKS-74U. This is especially useful for North Korea's SOF, which would typically be expected to have to engage in close quarters combat after their deployment to the densely urbanised South.

Both the regular Type-88 and its carbine variant were developed further during the late 2010s, ultimately spawning designs that look quite modern due to the adoption of new stocks, pistol grips and Picatinny-type rails for mounting accessories. Despite these ergonomical enhancements, no functional modifications to the rifles are apparent. Nevertheless, their sudden appearance alongside a range of different types of attachments during the 75th anniversary of the Workers' Party of Korea parade in 2020 could bring about a significant increase in effectiveness of elite troops and special forces, which had so far always relied on iron sights for targeting. It may be deduced that, while attempting to introduce a variety of new optics and other accessories to legacy weapons like the Type-88 it was found that the hassle of attempting to find a workaround to its lack of attachment points posed a greater challenge than simply introducing a new rifle variant. As a result, some optics (such as the LPS 4×6° TIP2 copy) are side mounted or even placed awkwardly on the Type-88's upper handguard for older models, and simply attached to the rails on newer ones. Meanwhile, Kim Jong Un's bodyguards have been spotted with Type-88s whose rear sights were modified to accommodate a compact, fixed red dot sight. The flood of new types of optics, including telescopic sights (mounted on marksman rifles, assault rifles, carbines and even SMGs), thermal scopes and red dot sights (one of which closely resembling the Russian EKP-1S-03) came paired with copious amounts of tactical flashlights, laser indicators, foregrips and most notably, suppressors. Four different variants of the latter entered service, one each for the marksman rifle, assault rifle, carbine and SMG that now equip the KPA's infantry. Their effectiveness has yet to be demonstrated however, and there are some indications that some of the types displayed were in fact mock-ups. While this also casts some doubt on the authenticity of the flood of new optics identified in recent years, it should be noted that North Korean indigenous optics go back a long way. Despite being an exceedingly rare sight, both copies of foreign designs and completely indigenous types (like the 'Night Scope-5', a compact night vision scope thought to date back to the 1980s) have long been found in the hands of infiltrators. Moreover, the recent iterations can often trace back their design to either these earlier optics or foreign types, providing a plausible technological origin.

The large size of the helical magazines means soldiers now have to grab the magazine instead of the handguard when aiming down the sights, likely resulting in decreased accuracy over longer ranges. (KCBC)

The newest iteration of the AK-74 in KPA service. This particular rifle is fitted with a 40mm GP-25 under-barrel grenade launcher, a bulky telescopic sight attached to the Picatinny-type rails, a large suppressor and a new lightweight plastic magazine and furniture. (KCBC)

Amongst the wealth of new armament unveiled during the 75th anniversary of the Workers' Party of Korea parade in 2020 were some that more radically departed from the AK-74's original design. One of the more striking amongst these is what at first glance would appear to be an entirely new bullpup assault rifle. Looks are deceiving however, and the bullpup conversion of AK-pattern rifles is relatively simple to achieve and popular not only among ex-Soviet countries, but even workshops in war-torn Syria. In its North Korean incarnation, very little of the Type-88s core workings were modified with the exception of the trigger assembly, which was moved to the front of the weapon. Its furniture was adapted accordingly, with the typical shoulder guard mated directly to the receiver, a carrying handle with Picatinny-type rails introduced above the upper handguard and a pistol grip and foregrip below the barrel. The result is a much shorter weapon than the Type-88, for the same barrel length and overall function. It is therefore the weapon of choice to be equipped with suppressors (of the same type sometimes seen on the KPA's marksman rifles during parades), and features often in video footage of SOF units. Though it represents one of the more atypical small arms introductions of the past decades, bullpups have some significant drawbacks due to the proximity of the receiver to the user's face and the location of the trigger, and many militaries worldwide have therefore slowly moved away from the concept in the recent past. North Korea's adaptation is thought to be no exception in terms of these limitations.

The Type-88 was to receive another radical modification in the form of the 'NK11' multi-weapon, in a development clearly inspired by South Korea's modern small arms industry.[37] Featuring the exact same layout as the troubled S&T Daewoo K11, which was developed in the 2000s as an advanced multi-barrelled weapon for the ROK Army, the North Korean weapon, which was first showcased

A SOF soldier grips his bullpup rifle. Note the telescopic sight, suppressor, under-barrel flashlight and side-mounted laser indicator. (KCBC)

during the 105th anniversary of the birth of Kim Il Sung parade in April 2017, combines a modified 5.45x39mm Type-88 with a magazine-fed grenade launcher of unknown calibre. Despite using different base designs and calibres for the assault rifle and grenade launcher components, virtually all design aspects seem to have been copied from the K11, including the bullpup-operation of the grenade launcher, its integration with the assault rifle and the stock of the weapon. What makes the South Korean design truly unique however, is its sophisticated ballistics computer and laser rangefinder (LRF) incorporated into its bulky sight, which enables it to select one of three fuses used by the 20mm grenades, thus detonating them in airburst mode, on contact or on contact with a delay – allowing it to first penetrate obstacles. Even though the North Korean weapon features a similarly bulky sight, it seems unlikely that it matches the K11's advanced options both in its ballistics computer or munition, although a LRF does appear to be fitted. Furthermore, the South Korean design was plagued by problems with the fire control system and firepower of the 20mm grenades and is prohibitively expensive, and was cancelled as a result. It is possible the North Koreans fared better by simplifying the design and its advanced features, and based on parade footage at least 800 were in service by September 2018. Nevertheless, a less complicated weapon forgoing the assault rifle component entirely was soon introduced, with first examples showcased during the parade marking the 8th Congress of the Workers' Party of Korea in January 2021. Utilising a broadly similar sight with integrated fire control system, it constitutes a fairly simple, bolt-action bullpup design, with a large gunstock and conspicuous muzzle break. Less versatile but also less flawed conceptually than the new multi-weapon, light grenade launchers such as these effectively bridge the gap between conventional rifles and heavier (single shot) grenade launchers that are also entering service.

The 'NK11' multi-weapon combines a modified 5.45x39mm Type-88 with a magazine-fed grenade launcher of unknown calibre. (NK Pro)

In parallel with ongoing efforts to further refine the time-honoured AK-74 design through the introduction of new Type-88 iterations and the development of a bullpup variant, the KPAGF is already looking ahead to the future. In 2023, Kim Jong Un was observed inspecting a completely new assault rifle design, marking the first North Korean assault rifle not rooted in the Kalashnikov lineage. Rather, this rifle closely resembles the design and appearance of the Belgian FN SCAR, down to individual design details of the

SOF soldiers in ghillie suits with the new bolt-action grenade launcher. Further down the row soldiers are carrying light rocket launchers with PG-7 munitions. (KCBC)

receiver. Like the SCAR, it comes chambered in two calibres, which are believed to be 5.45×39mm and 7.62×39mm so as to preserve commonality with previous generations of assault rifles. With the gradual introduction of elements of Western equipment in the late 2010s and 2020s the use of 5.56×45mm NATO cannot be excluded either however, especially given indications new assault rifles in 5.56×45mm NATO are being considered for adoption. Although the SCAR-H opted for the much more powerful 7.62x51mm cartridge, it appears North Korea did not follow suit with a copy or the comparable 7.62x54mmR. Similarly, there is as yet no indication that the ability to quickly exchange the barrel for a shorter or longer variant was copied over from the SCAR. Given that the next generation of infantry small arms will also require replacements for carbine and marksman rifles, this design feature should be highly attractive to the KPA. The new rifle is equipped with a Picatinny-type rail on the top of the receiver, along with two side rails and a bottom one, allowing for the attachment of various accessories, such as a foregrip or grenade launcher, and it seems even a bayonet lug was included. The ergonomics have seen a significant upgrade from the legacy Type-88 design, with the inclusion of a lightweight buttstock and a plastic magazine (a helical magazine is available as well). It remains unclear whether this rifle is a finalised design or one of several options being considered for adoption by the KPA, a pattern often observed with North Korean small arms designs. Certainly, the necessity to completely retool its legacy small arms factories in order to widely adopt the new generation will be a significant obstacle. Upon adoption, the new rifle will greatly benefit from a wide range of new optics and accessories currently being introduced by North Korea for its small arms designs.

A new assault rifle more immediately suited for wide-scale introduction was unveiled in mid 2024. Initially only shown as a prospective design on (blurred) posters at development institutes, at a SOF drill in September 2024 the weapon was first displayed in more detail, revealing that it is patterned closely after the Russian AK-12. Barring a number of mostly cosmetic differences, its structure is largely identical, including the full-length Picatinny rail, rear-mounted sights, muzzle brake, and even the ambidextrous fire selector that was introduced to the AK-12 in 2023. While it thus benefits from some (though not all) of the latest improvements to that weapon resulting from use in the Russo-Ukrainian War, improvements over new-built Type-88s are relatively modest. Its ergonomics and possibly build quality will likely compare favourably, while the option to utilise a foregrip or bipod are a boon to its versatility. Like other modern North Korean assault rifles, the ability to use a bayonet, helical magazine or under-barrel grenade launcher is retained, while a new optic resembling a Vortex Strike Eagle 1-8x24 was shown mounted. In a significant departure from previous practices, a variant chambered in 5.56×45mm NATO has also been developed, possibly on the basis of the Russian AK-19. Whether it, like the AK-19, is developed for export, or for an actual introduction into the KPA, remains unknown. However, the display of a carbine variant at the 'National Defence Development-2024' exhibition with side-folding stock and red dot sight is notable given that a 5.45×39mm carbine offshoot has not yet been displayed.

The new type of assault rifle unveiled in 2023 bears a close resemblance to the Belgian FN SCAR. The optic used seems to be patterned after the South Korean DI Optics PVS-11K. (KCBC)

The DPRK's new 5.56×45mm assault rifle at the 'National Defence Development-2024' exhibition. In the background, the carbine variant with side-folding stock. (KCBC)

Less ostentatious introductions of new armament may effect a greater change in capabilities in the KPA at a lower cost, and indeed there have been numerous such developments since the start of the 2000s. One example is a copy of the Soviet PG-7VR tandem warhead for the Type-68 RPG which is specifically designed to defeat ERA. By using a small shaped-charge that detonates the ERA so that the main charge can penetrate the armour behind it. While its cost and relatively niche role have so far prohibited wide-scale introduction into militaries around the world, the disparity between tanks of both sides means anti-armour equipment has received increasing funding in the DPRK. Only the ROKA K2 tank can make use of ERA thus far however, and inexplicably the first sighting of the North Korean variant of the PG-7VR during the parade for the 100th anniversary of Kim Il Sung's birthday in 2012 actually predates this tank's production. Another acquisition instead expanding on anti-infantry capabilities was of an unknown number of RPO-A Shmel disposable rocket launchers. These single-shot weapons usually fire thermobaric warheads, although incendiary or smoke-producing warheads can also be used, which work by dispersing a fuel into the air upon detonation. The subsequent ignition of this cloud of fuel results in an explosion that uses the oxygen in the air as oxidiser, thereby releasing more energy than a conventional explosive and depriving the area of oxygen. Relatively compact for the power it delivers, the RPO-A serves as a great addition to other infantry support weapons like light and heavy mortars, the AGS-17 AGL and its North Korean copy (whose production dates back to 1997), and flamethrowers such as the LPO-50 also in KPA service.

A uniquely North Korean invention aimed at further increasing the firepower of its soldiers at low cost consists of a stand-alone rocket launcher. Spotted in the hands of Kim Jong Un during various phases of its development at the start of the 2010s, it consists of a simple gun-type design that uses dummy cartridges to expel various types of rocket-propelled grenades. Perhaps the most interesting feature of this weapon is the fact that its munitions are compatible with the ubiquitous RPG-7. The booster charge which usually expels the rocket from the launcher is simply swapped for an inert one with only the stabilising fins, resulting in a simple, long-ranged indirect fire weapon with low accuracy. For this purpose, a telescopic sight not unlike the RPG-7's was fitted to the launcher, although the presence of a top-folding stock on one of the variants also indicates it is sometimes fired from the hip. When fired at a large angle, the weapon may be able to achieve ranges of over one kilometre, a substantial improvement over rifle grenades and other grenade launchers which typically are only effective out to a few hundred metres, and with a lighter payload. Of course, the weapon likely suffers from horrendous accuracy at such ranges due to its method of operation, and the costs of each individual round are much higher. While regular RPG warheads can be used in conjunction with the launcher, at least four types of warheads have specifically been designed for it, including high explosive (HE), fragmentation and incendiary. At least two of these variants have been exported to Cuba in the early to mid 2010s, and Sudan's Military Industry Corporation (MIC) now offers very similar projectiles.[38] Regular RPG-7 munitions such as the armour piercing PG-7 are also compatible (without booster), making this project very efficient in terms of the establishment of new production lines and logistics. Use of inert PG-7s with this weapon during parades suggest that North Korea indeed intends to use it in the anti-tank role at very short ranges.

Kim Jong Un wields a new AK-12/19-based assault rifle during SOF exercises in September 2024. (KCBC)

Roughly the same length as an average North Korean soldier, the Type-68 RPG equipped with a copy of the PG-7VR tandem warhead is a serious threat to even the most modern tanks in service today. (KCBC)

Kim Jong Un inspects an early prototype of the stand-alone rocket launcher. One of the at least four known warheads used in conjunction with the rocket launcher can be seen in front. (KCBC)

In the category of personal defence or infiltration-specific weapons, AFV crewmen and special forces in the past had to make do with pistols and SMGs like the Czechoslovakian Škorpion vz. 61 and a North Korean derivative (likely rechambered) – or in more recent years carbine variants of the Type-88. Yet the onslaught of new small arms unveiled during the parades of the late 2010s and early 2020s would include something to suit their needs. First seen during the 75th anniversary of the Workers' Party of Korea parade in 2020, the new SMG seemingly has a high degree of commonality with the Type-88, but is instead chambered in the 9×19mm Parabellum calibre that is also thought to be used by the Paektusan pistol.[39] With its apparent straight blowback operation, Picatinny-type rails, fastened-together double box magazines and modernised furniture it shares a very close likeness with the Russian PP-19 Vityaz, and certain of its external characteristics strongly suggest the Vityaz indeed served as the basis of the design. A dedicated compact telescopic sight and suppressor were developed, with the presence of a battery holder on the former implicating it projects a red dot on the reticle.

Aside from investments in weaponry, there are numerous other projects currently underway to improve the personal equipment of the KPA's soldiers. The early 2010s also saw a reimagining of the soldiers' combat uniform with a distinct US flavour, most notably by the introduction of camouflage uniforms patterned after the US designed M81 'Woodland' camouflage pattern, supplementing the olive drab green standard combat uniform in use since the 1950s. A variety of different colour schemes used to supplement the forest green have resulted in a broad family of uniforms currently entering service in large numbers. Most of these patterns are digital and come in a multitude of colour variations. The utilisation of a wide range of patterns indicates the absence of a definitive uniform, suggesting instead the adoption of multiple patterns to replace the olive drab green and M81 Woodland uniforms. Interestingly, some of these are reserved for specific branches, with the Missile General Bureau, Special Operations Force and border guards, as well as military police at the Joint Security Area (JSA), using uniquely coloured patterns and shoulder patches – another recent introduction. The SOF was previously the only branch to make wide-scale usage of camouflage uniforms, and by virtue of their importance it uses the largest variation of patterns. This applies to the border guards as well, which in addition to different colour schemes now also use a unique camouflage pattern that appears to be influenced by the British DPM camouflage pattern. Troops under the Ministry of Social Security are identifiable by their plain black uniforms, allowing for easy differentiation from their comrades within the KPA. For

Kim Il Sung inspects the personal equipment of a soldier in the early days of the KPA. (KCBC)

KPA elite forces with the new SMGs and body armour. Unlike other KPA soldiers, they also carry handguns and grenades. Note the Picatinny-type rails with laser indicator, flashlight and compact telescopic optics attached, as well as the specialised suppressor. (KCBC)

Almost half a century after the photo of Kim Il Sung was taken, Kim Jong Il and Kim Jong Un inspect newly introduced camouflage uniforms and tactical vests. (KCBC)

winter situations, some units are issued winter and snow woodland-style camouflage patterns and plain white parkas. Most recently camouflage patterns either inspired by or directly copied from the US's MultiCam and digital patterns like the South Korean Granite-B (of which some sections of pattern in fact correspond precisely) have been introduced in a variety of different colour schemes.

Introduced alongside the new camouflage uniforms are new helmets modelled after the popular US PASGT series of helmets, supplementing the various types of Soviet helmets and their North Korean copies still widely in use with the KPA. First seen paraded through the streets of Pyongyang during the 100th anniversary parade for Kim Il Sung's birthday in 2012, initial batches of these combat helmets might have been acquired from China, but in order to equip even a portion of the KPA indigenous production is a necessity, which seemed to be well underway by the early 2020s. The PASGT series has been supplemented in production by the US FAST helmets, which thus far have seen limited deployment among North Korean SOF units. Other improvements that have largely remained limited to North Korea's SOF and elite units are tactical vests and flak jackets, as well as simple night vision devices. At least a portion of this equipment is believed to have been sourced from China, as their acquisition is a relatively inexpensive method of expanding the efficacy of its SOF.

A number of more elaborate attempts are also being undertaken to increase the fighting efficacy of the KPA on the whole through the development of electronics such as battlefield surveillance radars and advanced Command, Control, Communications, Computers, Intelligence, Surveillance and Reconnaissance (C4ISR) equipment. The GD-200 is a man-portable surveillance and target acquisition radar that detects and measures the coordinates of ground vehicles within 10 kilometres and infantry within four kilometres in all weather conditions. Outwardly similar to and clearly derived from the Soviet PSNR-5 battlefield surveillance radar, the GD-200 is believed to have been developed along with a host of other battlefield surveillance and artillery locating radars, a number of which actually entered service with the KPA. Secure C4ISR equipment is thought to be far more prevalent amongst North Korean SOF than the rest of the military, with older types of electronics continuously being passed on to poorer funded units as new generations become available to the SOF. North Korean investment in this area is extolled in detail by its electronics exports through the Glocom front company (which according to its website was established in 1996), which markets a GS-2500 C4ISR Soldier System – alongside other naval, airborne and land-based assets part of the encompassing GS-2000 C4ISR System – meant to provide secure communication, combat orientation and even monitor individual soldiers' vitals.[40] Although Glocom mostly markets its products abroad, with many of the systems it advertises not entering service with the KPA, increasing numbers of radio packs, handheld radios and even communications devices with touchscreens are displayed during parades. Nevertheless, the fact that such equipment is expensive and in the past relied on foreign components means their battlefield impact might as yet remain limited. Glocom's export-oriented mission may well be aimed at offsetting its development costs, to some success. A shipment of 45 boxes of communications equipment manufactured by Glocom that was headed to Eritrea was intercepted in July 2016.[41] While it is uncertain if other shipments to Eritrea made it through, in a twist of irony the Ethiopian military was confirmed to make use of Glocom equipment in 2022.[42] Claims that Glocom has exported its GS-3100 Headquarters C4I System to at least one foreign customer suggest that significant exports have flown under the radar.

Even though in typical KPA fashion none of the aforementioned newly developed weaponry and equipment will actually replace any of the older designs, instead merely supplementing them, these new developments in North Korea's conventional assets are highly significant to its actual warfighting capabilities. It remains easy to mistake the KPA for an obsolete fighting force, completely incapable of replacing its outdated inventory – be it tanks and aircraft or simple small arms. In reality, innovation is proceeding at an increasing speed, and the plethora of new small arms and infantry equipment showcased in recent years serve as a stark reminder of the fact that North Korea has not yet run out of tricks up their sleeve. While small arms are a lot less intimidating and headline-grabbing than their WMD-delivering larger cousins, they too indicate a continuing trend of modernisation in the North Korean military.

The man-portable GD-200X Battlefield Surveillance Radar currently offered for sale by North Korea via Glocom. The GD-200X is a lighter alternative to the GD-200 that appears to be of indigenous design. (Glocom)

In recent times, a wide range of modern small arms designs, largely rooted in legacy models, have been adopted for service. A variety of entirely new designs are slated to complement these in the coming decade. These artworks are not to scale representations.

1. Since the introduction of the first Type-88s in the late 1980s, the base design has undergone continuous incremental improvements, incorporating new stocks, magazines, pistol grips and handguards. Shown here is the latest (base) variant, featuring a top-folding stock, along with a helical magazine that holds over 150 rounds.
2. While the Type-88 continues to benefit from ongoing improvements, efforts are already underway to develop the country's next-generation assault rifle. One of the two showcased designs closely resembles the Belgian FN SCAR. Like the FN SCAR, it was designed with modularity in mind and is chambered in at least two calibres. It incorporates features typical of modern assault rifles, including Picatinny-type rails, a telescopic stock, and lightweight magazines.
3. North Korea's new assault rifle is set to be part of a family of rifles, featuring both short and long barrel variants, and potentially a carbine designated marksman variant as well.
4. Further developed versions of the Type-88 offer enhanced versatility through the adoption of new stocks, pistol grips, and Picatinny-type rails for accessories such as scopes, foregrips, and laser or flashlight attachments, giving them a modern look. These are frequently seen equipped with a copy of the 40mm GP-25 under-barrel grenade launcher, as shown here.
5. The bullpup conversion of the Type-88 represents one of North Korea's more unusual small arms developments in recent years. Suppressors seem to be a standard feature on these models, while Picatinny-type rails facilitate the attachment of extra accessories.
6. The Type-88 has been further developed into two carbine variants, with the most modern iteration shown here. This weapon benefits from a variety of new optics and accessories introduced over the past decade. These can be mounted on Picatinny-type rails located on top of the receiver, as well as on two side rails and a bottom rail on the handguard.
7. An earlier carbine variant of the Type-88 features a top-folding stock, a significantly shortened gas tube, barrel and muzzle brake. Here it is shown with a helical magazine specifically designed for the carbine variant of the Type-88, capable of holding at least 80 rounds.
8. Unveiled for the first time in 2020, this submachine gun bears a striking resemblance to the Russian PP-19 Vityaz and appears to be based on its design. It likely utilises the 9×19mm Parabellum calibre, fed by double box magazines that are fastened together. A dedicated telescopic sight and suppressor were specifically designed for this weapon. These, along with other accessories, can be affixed to several Picatinny-type rails.
9. North Korea's RPK-74 copy featuring the same polymer furniture of the AK-74M, a side-folding stock and a new high-capacity casket magazine, likely holding 90 rounds, doubling the original capacity. (Artwork by Adam Hook)]

1
2
3
4
5
6
7
8
9
10
11
12

New advancements in weaponry have extended beyond just small arms designs. This artwork depicts various weapon types that have been designed or introduced into service in recent years. These artworks are not to scale representations.

1. Unveiled for the first time at the Self-Defence-2021 exhibition, a sniper rifle of similar appearance to the Accuracy International Arctic Warfare rifle. As this artwork is based on currently available imagery, its final form might differ from what can be seen here.
2. A new sniper rifle closely resembling the Russian DVL-10 M2. Kim Jong Un has reviewed and tested this rifle and a closely related variant on multiple occasions, indicating a probable future deployment within the KPA.
3. An anti-materiel rifle design reminiscent of the Russian KVSK. If the North decides to adopt this design, along with the aforementioned sniper rifles, it would address a notable gap in the KPA's arsenal, which is surprisingly devoid of sniper rifles. As this artwork is based on currently available imagery, its final form might differ from what can be seen here.
4. The 'NK11' multi-weapon has been put into service in significant quantities, a surprising development given the prohibitive costs and development challenges that prevented the US and South Korea from deploying similar arms.
5. A simpler weapon, omitting the assault rifle capability of the 'NK11' but retaining the bulky fire control system, has also been developed and adopted for service.
6. North Korea is a prolific user of the RPG-7 and its local variant, the Type-68. The introduction of a copy of the PG-7VR tandem warhead ensures these weapons remain potent against even tank armour fortified with ERA.
7. A stand-alone rocket launcher that can fire almost all types of rocket-propelled grenades compatible with the RPG-7, as well as several munitions specifically developed for it. Here, it is shown with a variant of the PG-7 grenade meant for use against tanks.
8. This new short-range ATGM shares many external characteristics with the Israeli Spike-SR fire-and-forget anti-tank system, and complements longer-ranged ATGMs like the Bulsae series and NLOS type missiles.
9. The HT-16PGJ MANPADS is an enhanced iteration of the 9K38 Igla that serves alongside a range of older MANPADS models. In the past decade, a more modern variant has emerged that seemingly still has to enter widespread service.
10. A unique development is this compact MANPADS, characterised by its shorter and wider dimensions, making it potentially easier for infantry to carry and possibly accommodating a larger warhead and/or seeker. As this artwork is based on currently available imagery, its final form might differ from what can be seen here.
11. This laser weapon is designed to cause blindness at distances of up to 1,500 metres. In 2003, reports emerged alleging North Korea's use of a laser gun to illuminate two US AH-64 Apache attack helicopters flying along the southern side of the DMZ. (Artwork by Adam Hook)]
12. North Korea has developed various countermeasures to combat enemy drones such as jammers as well as this drone gun designed to neutralise small civilian drones effectively within a range of two kilometres.

Fully kitted soldiers showcase the latest improvements in personal equipment, including local copies of the US FAST helmet and bullpup rifles. In reality, such equipment is mainly found in SOF units. (KCBC)

5
ARMOURED PERSONNEL CARRIERS

The KPA is traditionally an infantry-centred fighting force, with the bulk of personnel transported by truck, on tanks or simply afoot. Nevertheless, since the 1970s an increasing emphasis has been placed on APCs to provide a means of swiftly advancing alongside other mechanised units near the front lines. Like so many of its AFVs, North Korean APCs are specifically designed to exploit and overcome the peculiarities of the Korean Peninsula's mountainous and river-veined landscapes. Leaning on speed, mobility and above all the ability to cross bodies of water with little to no preparation required, they tend to combine a light APC design with relatively heavy firepower often in the form of a single or more commonly dual 14.5mm KPV heavy machine guns. Nevertheless, heavier armament often sported on today's APCs and IFVs such as autocannons and ATGMs are typically lacking, and their amphibiousness comes at the cost of very thin armour. For heavier fire support they therefore still rely on infantry and accompanying AFVs; true IFVs which are usually considered to carry larger calibre weaponry are scarce, with a plethora of fire support vehicles filling in the gap. Although production of tracked APCs first took off in earnest during the 1970s, a new wheeled family is now being introduced bringing the total number of APCs available to roughly 2,600 and rising. Certainly not all APCs were domestically produced however, and North Korea's affiliation with them can be traced back much further than its indigenous efforts at manufacturing them.

Even though a handful of APCs were in service with the KPA after the end of the Korean War, the DPRK placed little to no value on APCs in their infantry- and tank-centred army until the late 1960s. In the meantime, only scarce reports of deliveries of BTR-40s, BTR-152s and BTR-50s exist, with the latter two never having been seen in North Korean service. Only during the late 1960s, when both the indigenous artillery industry and tank industry started to see the light of day, did the need for APCs arise in order to transport infantry to the front lines alongside the newly mechanised forces. During this time the Soviet Union started delivery of amphibious BTR-60PB APCs, which North Korea claims to have copied by 1969 under the designation 69.[1] However, considering the relatively low number of BTR-60PBs currently in service with the KPA and the technological difficulties this would imply, it is more likely that these vehicles were assembled from SDKs, or that the claim is simply nonsense. A few years later, at the turn of the decennium, China began delivery of large amounts of amphibious 'Type 63' YW531A APCs. These vehicles would quickly be supplemented by an indigenous derivative, perhaps one of the most famous North Korean fighting vehicles in use with the KPA today. Commonly, yet incorrectly known as the VTT-323, this APC is referred to as the 323 in North Korea and has supposedly been in production since 1973 at the Sinhung armour plant.[2] Possibly produced with assistance from China, the most significant difference between the 323 and the YW531A is the addition of a turret wielding two 14.5mm KPV heavy machine guns and an optical device. This required the chassis to be lengthened by one road wheel, due to which the overall personnel-carrying capacity has not decreased, with North Korean sources even claiming 12 occupants.[3] Another significant improvement comes in the form of water jets, allowing the 323 to move through bodies of water much quicker than the YW531A, which uses its tracks to propel itself. Also notable is the fact that the 323 has two firing ports on either side, which appear to be copies of the same firing ports also seen on the BTR-60PB. The basic APC variant remained virtually unchanged throughout its production run, although in modern times a rare modification sports a 30mm AGL mounted in the right side of the turret. This addition does much to enhance the efficacy of the 323's armament, primarily increasing its ability to suppress opposing forces even without a line of sight. Interestingly, the 60th anniversary parade of the Korean People's Army in 1992 displayed the vehicle armed with a quadruple MANPADS launcher which had been slaved to the twin 14.5mms. Another variant is described by

323 APCs seen equipped with quadruple MANPADS launchers during the 1992 parade commemorating the 60th anniversary of the Korean People's Army. The degree of actual functionality of this variant is unknown. (KCBC)

A 323-based command vehicle, sporting more advanced communications equipment, a relatively spacious interior and loudspeakers to address nearby infantry. (KCBC)

With no direct replacement in sight, the 323 continues to soldier on as the KPAGF's primary armoured personnel carrier. In contrast with most other North Korean designed AFVs, the design of the 323 has remained virtually unchanged since its production run in the early 1970s. This may indicate that the DPRK remained satisfied with the original design during the following decades, which was superior over the US M113 APC used by the ROKA in terms of firepower and amphibious capabilities. (Artwork by David Bocquelet)

the US DoD as carrying two unspecified MANPADS and a Malyutka ATGM. Neither variant has ever been spotted in operational capacity, and due to the difficulties associated with operating the MANPADS from within the turret it is likely that they are in fact for display purposes only. Despite its extensive modifications, drawbacks from the original design of the YW531A remained such as the relatively thin armour coverage – providing protection for 12.7mm rounds at its thickest point – cramped interior and the fact that exiting the vehicle is only possible through a tiny rear door (smaller than on the YW531A due to the water jets) lacking a rear folding ramp and, with some effort, two rooftop hatches. This shortcoming was partially addressed by a variant that exchanged firepower for larger infantry carrying capabilities, forgoing the twin KPV turret for a single pintle-mounted KPV near the front of the vehicle. With its double rear doors it might actually have been a more capable APC, albeit one much less capable in the water due to a lack of waterjets, yet it appears to have been produced in limited capacity only nonetheless, serving mainly as the basis of other types of vehicles that use the 323 chassis. Despite its drawbacks, the standard 323 would be produced in great numbers, exported to Zimbabwe in 1984 and Ethiopia before 1987, and form the template for many fighting vehicles in a range of different roles.[4 5]

Persistent claims of some 100 BMP-1s being delivered during the 1972–1973 time period, and sometimes an additional 122 in the late 1980s, also appear in many sources, which also almost invariably mention the type is designated 'Korshun' in North Korea. This nickname, which is actually Russian for 'kite' – a bird species – is certainly incorrect, and no footage of these elusive IFVs in North Korean service exists. These rare vehicles do indeed appear to be in use to this day, albeit in far smaller numbers than reported. Accordingly, the BMP-1 seems to have had little impact on the DPRK's indigenous designs, and induced no desire to operate IFVs in any significant quantities. Instead, the 323 was deemed satisfactory and became the most prevalent APC design, albeit amongst a quantity of other rarer indigenous and foreign designs.

The development of one such different, wheeled APC design started much later: the first examples were seen during the 1992 parade commemorating the 60th anniversary of the Korean People's Army, receiving the US DoD designation of M-1992. This rather crude 4x4 vehicle, likely constructed with speed and manoeuvrability in mind, comes in at least three different variants. The basic APC variant, clearly inspired by the Soviet BRDM-1 amphibious scout car, could carry roughly six to eight personnel in addition to two crew members, and was equipped with a 30mm AGS-17 AGL and a 9K111 Fagot ATGM mounted on the passenger compartment. Although the vehicle is fully amphibious, it does not appear to be equipped with a water jet and thus has to propel itself through bodies of water using its tires. The production run of the M-1992 is thought to have been very limited, and outside of the 1992 parade it has not been seen in operational capacity.

An M-1992 APC during the 1992 parade commemorating the 60th anniversary of the Korean People's Army. Note the AGS-17 AGL and 9K111 ATGM. (KCBC)

In the meantime, the 323 slowly became outdated by modern APC standards, and it became clear a new design was required to match developments in the South such as the 6x6 K806 and 8x8 K808 wheeled APCs which are currently entering service. The 2000s heralded such a new generation of APC designs in North Korea, one that has been relatively poorly documented in Western sources. Starting with the delivery of a limited number of Russian amphibious BTR-80As, arguably – due to its 30mm autocannon – the only IFV other than the BMP-1 confirmed to be in KPA service the technology present in these wheeled 8x8 vehicles would soon be incorporated in the North's indigenous derivatives. Considering the limited number of examples acquired, the motivation behind the original purchase of BTR-80As was likely mainly to get access to the technology they contained as part of a Russian agreement for 'cooperation in the areas of defence industry and military equipment' signed in 2001.[6] Indeed, it is believed the first variant of what has been ascribed the US DoD designation 'M-2010' was conceived not long after the delivery of the BTR-80As. This BTR-like vehicle, which we will call the 8x8 M-2010-I here, best described as an amalgam of the BTR-60PB, BTR-80 and North Korean 323 APCs as well as the PT-76B light tank, was first spotted during the parade for the 65th anniversary of the Workers' Party of Korea in 2010 alongside its redesigned brethren. This amphibious 8x8 APC sports a turret inspired by that of the 323 APC, housing the same twin 14.5mm KPVs as its main armament, yet differing significantly from its ancestor by the addition of a coaxial 7.62mm coaxial machine gun, 2x3 smoke grenade dischargers, an infrared (IR) searchlight, a compact panoramic sight and a hatch for the operator. The M-2010 also features nuclear, biological, chemical (NBC) protection, the ventilation system of which takes up a substantial part of the rear of the turret. Much of the chassis is similar to that of the BTR-80, but when examining it in detail a myriad of differences come to light. Most notably, the 8x8 M-2010-I variant appears to use the PT-76B's 240hp diesel engine and associated water jets to propel itself on land and through water. Additionally, it uses BTR-60-style firing ports as opposed to the more practical ones found on the BTR-80, although later production batches did include this much improved design.

BTR-80A IFVs on parade. Although it is based on an APC chassis, these vehicles acquired only in limited numbers from Russia are designated IFVs by the virtue of their 30mm autocannon. (KCBC)

The 6x6 M-2010 APC's exhausts and water jets, which are identical to those of the PT-76B. (NK Pro)

A 6x6 derivative of the 8x8 M-2010-I also exists, likely fulfilling the reconnaissance role. Similar in many aspects to the 8x8 M-2010-I, the 6x6 M-2010 retains the same turret, engine and waterjets, but also incorporates new features that would later be seen on the 8x8 M-2010-II APC. Two of the front wheels were removed, and as a result the turret is now located directly over the side doors, limiting the size of the infantry compartment to roughly three or four passengers instead of seven. Since the engine has remained the same, the significant weight reduction brought on by this resizing likely does much to improve its mobility, providing a very fast troop transport/reconnaissance vehicle. Parade footage taken during the parade for the 90th anniversary of the Korean People's Revolutionary Army in April 2022 suggests that a number of these vehicles in dark camouflage are also in use with the Ministry of Social Security.

The new generation APC family reached its maturity with what will be referred to here as the 8x8 M-2010-II APC, a vehicle that is outwardly very similar to the original 8x8 M-2010-I but in fact incorporates several important modernisations. Most notably, the degree of commonality with the BTR-80 APC has progressively increased as factories became ready to incorporate new technologies, quite possibly to the degree of sharing the BTR-80A's 240hp diesel engine, as evidenced by the new BTR-80-style waterjet and exhausts. This means it is likely to be more reliable, have a better fuel economy and therefore larger operational range, not to mention better amphibious capabilities. Various other modifications, presumably to the interior as much as to the exterior, make up the rest of the differences between the two variants, but the new engine remains the most notable. In many of its capabilities, the 8x8 M-2010, and especially the second variant, will be much akin to the BTR-80 family of APCs. Although it is more crudely finished, it packs greater firepower and together with its 6x6 offshoot offers an interesting degree of versatility. No matter how sizeable the total production run however, it is evident the M-2010 family as always will only supplement APCs currently in use, and in accordance with KPA doctrine in other branches practically all APC types ever delivered remain in use.

In this image one of the later generation M-2010 APCs is used to carry the casket of Marshal Ri Ul Sol during his state funeral in 2015. Note that the 2x14.5mm armament has been removed, and that this variant sports the upgraded engine and accompanying BTR-80-style water jet. (NK Pro)

Farther to the rear, transportation both of infantry and supplies occurs mainly by truck, jeep or train. With the latter particularly vulnerable to enemy air power, unarmoured wheeled transportation vehicles too have received much attention in recent years. Soviet-legacy examples such as the ubiquitous ZiL-130, ZiL-131, ZiL-157 and KrAZ-255B trucks and UAZ-469 jeeps, supplemented by numerous indigenous trucks and jeeps of the Chaju, Sungri and Kaengsaeng brands as well as a number of West-German Mercedes-Benz 230G(E) jeeps and other vehicles produced by nations such as Romania, Japan, and East Germany, have been supplemented by increasing numbers of modern, mainly Chinese, newcomers. Although a large variety of Chinese trucks have been in service since the Cold War, numbers swelled after a 2011 acquisition of over 3,000 military vehicles, including large numbers of HOWO trucks and BAW jeeps.[7] Sporadic numbers of modern Russian vehicles, such as the ZiL-4334 4x4 truck and Taepaeksan-96 – which is a variant of the KamAZ-55111 assembled in North Korea in 2007 – cannot

A later generation 8x8 M-2010 APC. Note the BTR-80-style firing ports, and redesigned exhaust pipes. (NK Pro)

compete with these amounts, and modern unarmoured transports in the KPA are therefore predominantly Chinese. The difficulties in importing further trucks spurred on the development of an indigenous heavy truck industry however, and in recent years there has been a wild growth in new up-armoured platforms used to carry heavy weapons systems.

Another interesting new development is an infantry mobility vehicle first spotted during the parade for the 70th anniversary of the foundation of the DPRK in September 2018. Apparently based on a Chinese BAW jeep, it constitutes the sole vehicle of its type in the KPA, with other armoured cars such as the Second World War-era BA-64B scout car and the M-1992 APC being designed with different roles in mind. Armour thickness appears to be uniform and upwards of 10mm, providing sufficient protection from most small arms, and six smoke grenade dischargers fitted to the roof provide an additional degree of protection. Judging by badges affixed to the front and rear of the car, its North Korean designation seems to be 727 – after the date of the signing of the armistice on 27 July – and despite similarities with Chinese vehicles it does appear much of its components are indigenously manufactured. Although it is unlikely to have an impact as large as other newly introduced lines of AFVs, developments such as these show that the current push for modernisation is more than just a token effort, with resources being devoted to projects even when they serve little propaganda value.

More curious still, and seemingly introduced in larger numbers, is an infantry mobility vehicle (IMV) first displayed during the 75th anniversary of the Workers' Party of Korea parade in 2020 that bears more than a passing resemblance to the Japanese Komatsu LAV. Features of the Komatsu were copied down to surprising detail, save for the fact that no single feature precisely matches its inspiration. Despite its external similarities, shots of the interior show the vehicle was in fact adapted from the commercial Mitsubishi Pajero SUV, implying its likeness is the result of mimicry rather than a technological link. Assuming North Korea is not attempting to set up a production line for these cars, this means introduction of this IMV is limited to the amount of vehicles they can smuggle into the country, highlighting the importance of strict adherence to sanctions to limit innovation in the KPA.

Production of tracked APCs has not ceased entirely however, and the manufacture of a new tracked APC/reconnaissance vehicle design started in 2009.[8] This vehicle, designated the Chunma-D, is based heavily on the chassis of the Sinhung amphibious light tank, and might well have found its origin in an attempt to repurpose old Sinhung factory lines now that the type is no longer in production. Tellingly, it features little external modification aside from carrying a turret with two 14.5mm KPVs and a coaxial 7.62mm instead of the 85mm gun turret seen on the Sinhung. This turret, largely similar but not identical to the one seen on the M-2010, is located directly above the infantry compartment, which features two firing ports identical to those on the BTR-80 on either side and two-part doors which open partly through the side and the roof of the vehicle. The effectiveness of this vehicle as an APC is debatable, as its rear located engine leaves little room for infantry, which likely number four to six, and the side-facing doors are cumbersome to exit from swiftly. In fact, although it incorporates some new technologies bolted onto its hull that have become available since the inception of the 323 APC, its general layout and capabilities are either very similar or plainly inferior to the 323's, depending on the aspect considered. In this sense, the Chunma-D might well become a one-off comparable to the M-1992, enjoying a short production run possibly in a variety of roles for which it is not particularly well suited, possibly including a 30-barrel MRL variant. Its primary redeeming quality might well be the armour it inherited from the Sinhung's design, making this vehicle slightly more capable in an offensive role as opposed to the troop carrier task most APCs are relegated to.

Although better armed and armoured infantry carriers – such as the IFVs of which the South has increasingly many – are generally lacking in the KPA, this has not stopped it from developing its own entirely unique method of directly providing advancing mechanised forces with the ability to suppress enemy forces or destroy fortifications prior to an attack. As early as the 1970s APC-mounted MRLs started to appear, amongst which is one outfitted with the standard 3x4 107mm Type-63 MRL block. This early contraption was obviously very impractical due to its inability to rotate the MRL however, leading to the difficult situation where the entire vehicle had to be turned if it was misaligned with its target. All later variants therefore used a larger 3x6 – or in recent years 3x8 – MRL block on a rotating platform, for which a special broadened 323 chassis was developed. It is uncertain if it retains its infantry carrying abilities however, with firing ports conspicuously missing on this variant. If it does have capacity for passengers, it would constitute a unique APC design with the capacity to lay down a sizeable barrage of rocket fire on enemy positions before infantry storms them. Depending on the internal layout, additional reloads may or may not be carried inside, and their widespread deployment is liable to put a high strain on logistics. Nevertheless, this tactic is certain to require some careful consideration to successfully counter, and the shock value of such intense short-ranged bombardments must not be underestimated. Another, perhaps even more curious design again utilises the 323 to carry a 122mm MRL with two 2x3 blocks of launch tubes for a total of 12 rockets. These APCs, named the Sonyon ('Child', alluding to the fact that several batches have been 'donated' by schoolchildren) in North Korea, combine

The newly developed 727 infantry mobility vehicle seen during the 70th anniversary of the foundation of the DPRK parade in September 2018. (NK Pro)

Marshal of the Korean People's Army Ri Pyong Chol addresses the soldiers ahead of the January 2021 parade from a Komatsu LAV-inspired (and Mitsubishi Pajero-based) IMV. He would be stripped of his title later that year. (KCBC)

infantry carrying capabilities with relatively long-range MRL capabilities, making for a versatile yet very odd design choice all the same.[9] The installation of new BTR-80-style firing ports on examples delivered to the army in recent times indicate it indeed does not forgo its infantry carrying capabilities, and correspondingly it seems unlikely that it is capable of carrying any spares for its MRL. All the same, the concept of mechanised units in the field being capable of directly utilising their own carriers for instance in a limited counter-battery fire mission is exceptional and could be effective if combined with proper C4ISR practices.

Its designs of the past show that North Korea is well capable of surprises when it comes to the introduction of indigenous APCs, and as such the future may well hold unexpected turns of events. Although it may well for the moment feel content with continuing the M-2010 line, the DPRK is indubitably aware of developments in other nations, which tend to favour more armour and heavier armament than is customary on existing KPA designs. Therefore, especially the introduction of APCs/IFVs carrying autocannons, conceivably derived from the BTR-80A's 2A72, seems like a plausible future development, despite the current continued fixation on the 14.5mm KPV as the main armament on most vehicles. Still, at least at the moment the primary strategy appears to be to draw frontline firepower from dedicated support vehicles or tanks; APCs provide transportation to the front, where the most intense fights are slugged out by the infantry and its massive armoured forces.

A Chunma-D APC during the 100th anniversary of Kim Il Sung's birthday parade in 2012. Note the BTR-80-style firing ports. (David Flack)

Sonyon MRL-capable APCs roll down the streets of Pyongyang during the 70th anniversary of the foundation of the DPRK parade in September 2018. Note the BTR-80-style firing ports. (NK Pro)

6
FIRE SUPPORT VEHICLES

The 2020s would bring the first inklings of a departure from this strategy, with the introduction of a new wheeled platform used as a basis for several specialised AFVs including a fire support vehicle, mobile anti-tank missile system, and a command vehicle. Although similar in appearance to the M-2010 8x8 wheeled APC (which in turn derives in large part from the BTR-80), it features various crucial design differences that bring it more in line with Western vehicles like the Canadian LAV III. The most significant changes to that effect are large amounts of bolt-on armour, the abolition of firing ports, and (on some vehicles) the relocation of the engine towards the front in order to accommodate a large rear-facing door. This ensures greater survivability against heavy machine guns, anti-materiel rifles and HE shrapnel that may be encountered near the front lines, combining mobility and a moderate degree of protection with enhanced firepower to support infantry and other AFVs in the field. Nevertheless, they seem to lack amphibious capabilities beyond a waterproof hull and wheeled propulsion, and do not feature the V-shaped hull that has become common on modern wheeled platforms to enhance survivability against mines and improvised explosive devices (IEDs).

Two types of AFVs based on this platform were first displayed during the 75th anniversary of the Workers' Party of Korea parade in 2020. Perhaps the most striking of the two mimics the USA's M1128 Mobile Gun System by mating an unmanned turret (whose operators are located in an affixed segment embedded in the vehicle) housing a modified 122mm D-30 howitzer to the rear of the vehicle. Favoured in North Korea on a variety of self-propelled platforms, the D-30 has the ability to use HEAT and HE shells in direct-fire mode, thus making it suitable for this type of vehicle. To aid it in this capacity, a wind sensor and bulky gunner's optics were added to this turret alongside features standard among modern North Korean AFVs such as laser warning receivers (LWRs) and smoke grenade dischargers. For additional firepower, an AGL on the right hand side is operated by a crew member located below the turret. The M1128 MGS's defining technology is perhaps its autoloader however, which consists of a round ammo storage in the rear of the vehicle that can be aligned with a round magazine in the rotating section below the turret. A separate mechanism loads the rounds from the latter magazine up into the breech. Since the North Korean iteration features an additional crew member, such a complex system might not have been deemed necessary. Nevertheless, given that the turret itself is unmanned some degree of automation is evident. The question remains of how the North Korean design handles the D-30's two-piece munitions consisting of a separate loading charge and projectile. If the autoloader was designed to accommodate two-piece munitions, this would enhance the system's flexibility in firing missions at the cost of greatly increased complexity. Alternatively, the D-30 could have been modified for the use of specially-designed one-piece munitions. Though the addition of a bore evacuator to the barrel does indicate some changes to the howitzer, this would entail a far more extensive redesign and necessitate setting up a production line for an entirely new type of munition, both of which seem implausible.

To accommodate the turret and loading mechanism, the engine was moved from the rear to directly behind the front cabin of the vehicle, and the internal layout is therefore substantially different from the M-2010. Accordingly, the side-facing hatches were removed, and a rear-facing door to facilitate reloading and crew access was installed. With the engine now situated towards the front of the vehicle, amphibious propulsion beyond the momentum provided by the wheels is absent. Similarly, a lack of firing ports is a testament to the fact the M-2010's infantry carrying capabilities have been surrendered in favour of its role as fire support vehicle. Though questions about the vehicle's exact technical characteristics remain, there is little doubt that it constitutes a genuine development, albeit potentially one still under development. The same evaluation applies to other, less openly displayed vehicles based on the same platform, which are believed to include a spacious command vehicle with a forward-located engine and rear-facing door.

A different AFV unveiled in 2024 may well explain some of the more mysterious aspects of M1128 MGS-inspired design. Shown only as a large, desert-coloured scale model at the Academy of Defence Sciences, it utilises a chassis derived from the new 8x8 platform, with a substantially beefed up engine transplanting one of the crew members in the front

The M1128 MGS-inspired wheeled AFV. Note the conspicuous gunner's optic, and the exhaust betraying the fact that the engine has been relocated to the front of the vehicle. (KCBC)

A large scale model of the new wheeled mobile gun. In the back, the latest MBT, an indigenous tank engine derived from the MT 883, and the day and night optics associated with the same tank. (KCBC)

of the vehicle. More conspicuously, the unmanned turret with D-30 howitzer has been done away with entirely, and replaced by a very-large crewed-design that houses a large cannon, presumed 100mm but possibly even 115mm or 120mm in calibre. The turret features two crew hatches, gunner's day and night optics embedded on the left hand side, a remote weapon station (RWS) housing an AGL with integrated optics on the right, and a very large turret bustle to the rear for ammunition stowage to which six smoke grenade dischargers attach on either side. The cannon has many elements in common with the Chonma-2's main gun, including a muzzle reference device and compact LRF, but introduces a pepper pot muzzle brake. The LWRs that had become endemic to modern North Korean AFV designs have been replaced by new sensors more directly embedded in the turret. Though there is as yet no evidence of any prototypes of this vehicle that are to scale, it probably represents a more feasible and mature approach to a mobile gun system, while demonstrating the versatility of the new 8x8 platforms the KPA is set to introduce.

The same venue that had the new wheeled mobile gun on display also partially lifted the veil on the full extent of plans for this 8x8 wheeled AFV family. A conspicuously digitally obscured poster set out North Korea's ambitions for as many as 12 different AFVs, each centred around the same unified 8x8 chassis bearing a forward-located engine. While further details can only be guessed at, it appears the family encompasses several vehicles in addition to the 8x8 AFVs already publicly displayed since 2020, including an APC, self-propelled mortar (SPM), armoured recovery vehicle (ARV), and variant equipped with HMG or autocannon. Some of the vehicles, which come in desert or forest colour schemes, furthermore seem to bear an external resemblance to the South Korean K808 AFV family. It may well be that this family thus prompted the North Korean development programme, and serves as its inspiration. With so many designs as yet uncovered, it is certain that the next decade will see the unveiling of a large variety of new fighting vehicles, heralding an advance in its mechanised forces unseen since the 1970s.

Yet another new AFV that is at first sight very similar to the M1128 MGS-inspired design (and presumed part of this family despite its engine configuration) was also unveiled during the 75th anniversary of the Workers' Party of Korea parade in 2020. While it featured the same up-armoured 8x8 chassis as the fire support vehicle, instead it dons a remote turret with a quintuple pop-up ATGM launcher as its main armament. This launcher features five Bulsae-5 ATGMs and a sight containing the associated day/night optics and laser that guides the missiles. Affixed to the turret is also the same LWR and smoke grenade discharger-based passive protection system seen on virtually any new North Korean AFV. Unlike the M1128-inspired design however, the engine for this vehicle is still situated in the back, and operators for the ATGM system and AGL located in front of the turret are given access through a tiny hatch on the left hand side of the vehicle. The absence of an infantry carrying capability begs the question of what the remaining space in the interior is used for. One possibility is that it contains reloads for the ATGM turret, possibly with a system (either manual or automated) to reload the launcher from inside the vehicle. The high cost of North Korea's 9M133 Kornet-derived missile (offered for export for a whopping $53,000 US in 2017) is likely to make such a system uneconomical however, and a launcher with fewer missiles ready for launch would have made for a more sensible design if this were the case.[1]

Another recent development – and potentially a real knockout punch – is a new type of ATGM first displayed during the parade for the 70th anniversary of the foundation of the DPRK in September 2018. This ATGM carrier is based on the older 6x6 'M-2010' APC and features a large angular turret fitted with eight large missile canisters. The missiles themselves in appearance, dimensions and in basic operation closely resemble the Chinese CM-501GA land attack missile, featuring large collapsible fins and an imaging infrared (IIR) seeker in the nose. For targeting, what appears to be a battlefield surveillance radar is mounted to the rear, though remote spotters and user correction during flight can likely also be used. Such weapons are capable of engaging targets at extreme ranges and beyond the line of sight, an ability that is certain to be of use on the Korean Peninsula where hills and forests often obstruct the view. It is no coincidence that South Korea itself also operates the Israeli Spike NLOS (Non-Line-Of-Sight), for instance deploying them to Yeonpyeong Island after the bombardment of 2010. The North Koreans were doubtlessly aware of this fact, and the new ATGM would not be the first product whose development was apparently prompted by a reactionary request to match new South Korean acquisitions. If the Chinese CM-501GA indeed has a direct relation to the North Korean missile, then a range of up to 40 kilometres can be expected, with global navigation satellite system (GNSS) combined with IIR guiding its 20 kilogrammes of explosive payload to the target. Whatever the case, just like the Israeli Spike family North Korea clearly intends to use the system not just against land targets, with both a coastal defence variant based on a lightly armoured car with an integrated surface search radar as well as a navalised launch platform being introduced.

With the introduction of this missile seemingly accelerating, the KPA is quite suddenly in possession of multiple types of new generation guided weaponry that could be capable of dispensing with most types of weapons systems the ROK and USA currently field. This is in addition to a flood of loitering munitions unveiled in the mid 2020s, which will be discussed in more detail in the volume on the KPAAF. The NLOS missile's advanced capabilities indubitably make it one of the most potent weapons in the North's arsenal, and it is consequently attracted some foreign attention. Notably, in 2024 indications emerged that Russia had received at least some examples, and was utilising them in its conflict with Ukraine. Footage from spotter drones appeared to show multiple hits on Ukrainian artillery in March from a top-down attack munition that did not match known types. In July, a Ukrainian reconnaissance drone shot footage of an apparent 6x6 NLOS launcher behind Russian lines, with the vehicle reportedly firing six missiles before relocating.[2] It is possible that experience gained in Ukraine was directly applied to the continued production of this vehicle, with a variant displayed in November 2024 utilising a more spacious 8x8 APC for its chassis instead.

The new ATGM carrier with five Bulsae-5 missiles. The heavy bolted-on armour that gives the vehicle enhanced survivability in its combat role is readily apparent. (KCBC)

North Korea's NLOS-like missile is launched from its 6x6 launching platform, which has the capacity to carry up to eight of these missiles. Note the device to the rear of the vehicle, thought to be a battlefield surveillance radar. (KCBC)

NLOS-capable ATGM carriers paraded through the streets of Pyongyang. Note the grenade dischargers and LWR that make up the active protection system mounted to most new North Korean AFVs. (KCBC)

Armoured cars carrying the NLOS-capable missiles for use against naval targets. An integrated radome fitted to the rear aids it in target acquisition. (KCBC)

BIBLIOGRAPHY

Berger, Andrea. *Target Markets* (Abingdon: Routledge, 2015)

Bermudez Jr., Joseph S. *Shield of the Great Leader: The Armed Forces of North Korea* (St Leonards: Allen & Unwin, 2001)

Federal Research Division. *North Korea a country study* (Washington, DC.: Federal Research Division, 2008)

Gerardi, Greg J,. James A. Plotts. *An Annotated Chronology of DPRK Missile Trade and Developments* (Monterey: Nonproliferation Studies at the Monterey Institute of International Studies, 1994)

James Martin Center for Nonproliferation Studies at the Monterey Institute of International Studies *North Korea Missile Chronology* (Washington, DC.: Nuclear Threat Initiative, 2012)

Kim Il Sung, *The present situation and the tasks of our party; report at the conference of the Workers' Party of Korea* (Pyongyang: Foreign Languages Pub, 1966)

Korean Overseas Information Service. *Undermining Peace: North Korea's Infiltration Tunnels* (Seoul: Korean Overseas Information Service, 1991)

Marine Corps Intelligence Activity. *North Korea Country Handbook* (Quantico: Marine Corps Intelligence Activity, 1997)

Ministry of National Defence of the Republic of Korea. *Defense White Papers 2006-2018* (Yongsan, Seoul: Ministry of National Defence of the Republic of Korea, 2006-2018)

Sang-Hoon Chung, Joseph. *North Korea's "Seven Year Plan" (1961-70): Economic Performance and Reforms in Asian Survey Vol. 12 No. 6* (Berkeley: University of California Press, 1972)

Singlaub, John K. et al. *Hazardous Duty* (New York City: Touchstone, 1992)

Ustyantsev S. Kolmakov D. *T-72/T-90 Experience in developing domestic main battle tanks* (Nizhny Tagil: UVZ, 2013)

ENDNOTES

Preface

1 We forsook the opportunity to use KPAAAAAF.
2 Artworks in this book series serve mainly to elucidate subjects of which appropriate imagery is lacking, and as such certain volumes contain noticeably larger numbers of artworks than others.

Introduction

1 The total numbers of rounds fired at Yeonpyeong is often stated as 170, 150 of which were in the first barrage, whereas the three MRL batteries stationed on the Kangnyong Peninsula alone would likely have been capable of firing up to 1,440 122mm rockets within minutes, depending on the type of launchers involved.
2 Joseph S Bermudez Jr. 'The Yŏn-p'yŏng-do Incident' (2011) *38 North* https://www.38north.org/wp-content/uploads/2011/01/38North_SR11-1_Bermudez_Yeonpyeong-do.pdf

Chapter 1

1 In North Korea's account of history Kim Il Sung naturally plays a central role both in its foundation and leadership. It appears this narrative was highly embellished during the 1970s however, when celebration of the 8 February founding of the KPA ceased and propaganda about Kim Il Sung's heroic past became more pervasive.
2 Kathryn Weathersby. '"Should We Fear This?" Stalin and the Danger of War with America' (2002) *Wilson Center* https://www.wilsoncenter.org/publication/should-we-fear-stalin-and-the-danger-war-america
3 DPR Korea. 'Outstanding Leadership and Brilliant Victory' (1993) *Wilson Center* https://digitalarchive.wilsoncenter.org/document/155225
4 Central Intelligence Agency. 'National Intelligence Estimate Number 42.2-56 Probable Developments In North Korea Over The Next Few Years' (1956) *CIA FOIA* https://www.cia.gov/readingroom/document/0005500089
5 Kim Gwang-hyeop. 'TELEGRAM FROM PYONGYANG TO BUCHAREST, NO. 76.161 TOP SECRET, MAY 10, 1967' (1967) *Wilson Center* https://digitalarchive.wilsoncenter.org/document/116703
6 Joseph Sang-Hoon Chung. *North Korea's "Seven Year Plan" (1961-70): Economic Performance and Reforms* (Berkeley: University of California Press, 1972)
7 Mitchell Lerner. "Mostly Propaganda in Nature:' Kim Il Sung, the Juche Ideology, and the Second Korean War' (2010) *Wilson Center* https://www.wilsoncenter.org/publication/mostly-propaganda-nature-kim-il-sung-the-juche-ideology-and-the-second-korean-war
8 Central Intelligence Agency. 'US Helicopter Shot Down By South Koreans' (1974) *CIA FOIA* https://www.cia.gov/readingroom/document/cia-rdp78s01932a000100130014-9
9 Ria Chae. 'East German Documents on Kim Il Sung's April 1975 Trip to Beijing' (1975) *Wilson Center* https://www.wilsoncenter.org/publication/east-german-documents-kim-il-sungs-april-1975-trip-to-beijing
10 Heinz Hoffmann. 'Report on a Stay of a GDR Military Delegation in the DPRK in October 1976' (1976) https://digitalarchive.wilsoncenter.org/document/report-stay-gdr-military-delegation-dprk-october-1976
11 John K. Singlaub et al., *Hazardous Duty* (New York: Touchstone, 1992)
12 John K. Singlaub et al., *Hazardous Duty* (New York: Touchstone, 1992)
13 Steinhofer. 'REPORT FROM THE GDR EMBASSY IN THE DPRK' (1975) *Wilson Center* https://digitalarchive.wilsoncenter.org/document/114284
14 Steinhofer. 'REPORT FROM THE GDR EMBASSY IN THE DPRK' (1975) *Wilson Center* https://digitalarchive.wilsoncenter.org/document/114284
15 Andrei Gromyko. 'FROM THE JOURNAL OF GROMYKO, RECORD OF A CONVERSATION WITH AMBASSADOR RI SIN-PAL OF THE DEMOCRATIC PEOPLE'S REPUBLIC OF KOREA' (1958) *Wilson Center* http://digitalarchive.wilsoncenter.org/document/116019
16 Central Intelligence Agency. 'The Korean Military Balance And Prospects For Hostilities On The Peninsula' (1987) *CIA FOIA* https://www.cia.gov/readingroom/document/0005569324
17 János Taraba. 'REPORT, EMBASSY OF HUNGARY IN NORTH KOREA TO THE HUNGARIAN FOREIGN MINISTRY' (1985) *Wilson Center* https://digitalarchive.wilsoncenter.org/document/110142

Chapter 2

1 Korean Central News Agency. 'Kim Jong Un Guides Test-fire of Newly Developed Anti-tank Guided Weapon' (2016) *KCNA* www.kcna.co.jp/item/2016/201602/news27/20160227-01ee.html
2 The constitution was revised in 2019, replacing the previous title of 'Supreme Commander' with 'Commander-in-Chief.'
3 Technically the First Chairman, as the title of Eternal Chairman was posthumously awarded to Kim Jong Il.
4 Republic of Korea Ministry of National Defense. 'Defense White Papers 2006-2022' *ROK MoD*
5 Republic of Korea Ministry of National Defense. 'Defense White Papers 2006-2022' *ROK MoD*
6 Republic of Korea Ministry of National Defense. 'Defense White Papers 2006-2022' *ROK MoD*

7 North Korea Leadership Watch. 'KWP Central Committee Organization and Guidance Department' (2009) *North Korea Leadership Watch* https://nkleadershipwatch.files.wordpress.com/2009/10/kwpcentralcommitteeorganizationandguidancedepartment.pdf

8 North Korea Leadership Watch. 'State Security Department' *North Korea Leadership Watch* http://www.nkleadershipwatch.org/state-security-department/

9 BBC News 'North Korea defector numbers 'drop' under Kim' (2018) *BBC* https://www.bbc.com/news/world-asia-45697236

10 Republic of Korea Ministry of National Defense. 'Defense White Papers 2006-2022' *ROK MoD*

11 Ho Il Moon. 'How big is the North Korean army? Evidence from missing population' (2011) *VOX* https://voxeu.org/article/how-big-north-korean-army-evidence-missing-population

12 Republic of Korea Ministry of National Defense. 'Defense White Papers 2006-2022' *ROK MoD*

13 Rodong Sinmun. '"More Than 3 475 000 Korean People Volunteer to Join or rejoin in Army"' (2016) *Rodong Sinmun*

14 Choi Song Min. 'Mandatory Military Service Extends to Women' (2015) *Daily NK* https://www.dailynk.com/english/mandatory-military-service-extends/

15 Federal Research Division. *North Korea a country study.* (Washington, DC., Federal Research Division, 2008)

16 Federal Research Division. *North Korea a country study.* (Washington, DC., Federal Research Division, 2008)

17 Choi Song Min. 'Mandatory Military Service Extends to Women'

18 Known from 1972 until 2020 as the Ministry of People's Armed Forces.

19 Only three KPA branches existed during the Cold War, nowadays there are five.

20 Republic of Korea Ministry of National Defense. 'Defense White Paper 2018' *ROK MoD*

21 Republic of Korea Ministry of National Defense. 'Defense White Papers 2006-2022' *ROK MoD*

22 Republic of Korea Ministry of National Defense. 'Defense White Papers 2006-2022' *ROK MoD*

23 Joseph S. Bermudez Jr., *Shield of the Great Leader: The Armed Forces of North Korea* (St Leonards NSW: Allen & Unwin, 2001)

24 Republic of Korea Ministry of National Defense. 'Defense White Paper 2008' *ROK MoD*

25 Republic of Korea Ministry of National Defense. 'Defense White Papers 2006-2022' *ROK MoD*

26 Republic of Korea Ministry of National Defense. 'Defense White Papers 2006-2022' *ROK MoD*

27 The observant reader might have noticed the lack of a VI and XI Infantry Corps; the VI Corps was disbanded in 1995 and its units put under the command of the IX Corps after allegations of corruption or even a possible coup attempt by its commanders. The fate of the XI Corps is slightly more complex, and its name now lives on as a code name for the infamous Storm Corps – North Korea's premier SOF unit.

28 Joseph S. Bermudez Jr. 'KPA Journal Vol. 2 No.7' (2011) *KPA Journal* http://www.kpajournal.com/vol-2-no-7-july-2011/

29 Republic of Korea Ministry of National Defense. 'Defense White Papers 2006-2022' *ROK MoD*

30 Republic of Korea Ministry of National Defense. 'Defense White Papers 2006-2022' *ROK MoD*

31 Republic of Korea Ministry of National Defense. 'Defense White Papers 2006-2022' *ROK MoD*

32 Republic of Korea Ministry of National Defense. 'Defense White Papers 2006-2022' *ROK MoD*

33 Republic of Korea Ministry of National Defense. 'Defense White Papers 2006-2022' *ROK MoD*

34 Republic of Korea Ministry of National Defense. 'Defense White Papers 2006-2022' *ROK MoD*

35 GlobalSecurity.org 'Homeland Reserve Force' *GlobalSecurity* https://www.globalsecurity.org/military/world/rok/hrf.htm

36 Republic of Korea Ministry of National Defense. 'Defense White Papers 2006-2022' *ROK MoD*

37 Michael Ha. 'US to Deploy 690,000 to Korea in Emergency' (2008) *The Korea Times* https://www.koreatimes.co.kr/www/nation/2023/02/113_32934.html

38 Ruediger Frank. 'The SPA Session of April 2014: Spotlight on Sports and Economic and Trade Zones' (2014) *38 North* https://www.38north.org/2014/04/rfrank042314/

Chapter 3

1 Piro Bita and the DPRK Ambassador to Albania. 'Information on a Meeting between Piro Bita and the DPRK Ambassador' (1967) *Wilson Center* https://digitalarchive.wilsoncenter.org/document/114384

2 Kim Il Sung., *The Present Situation and the Tasks of Our Party* (Pyongyang: Foreign Languages Pub, 1966)

3 China has been actively training to take out North Korean military installations in the event relations with the DPRK turn sour. Amongst others, this has included training on securing a mock-up of the Yongbyon nuclear reactor and the adjacent river at the Taonan Combined Arms Tactical Training Ground in Jilin Province, Northeast China.

4 Joseph S. Bermudez Jr., *Shield of the Great Leader: The Armed Forces of North Korea* (St Leonards NSW: Allen & Unwin, 2001)

5 Republic of Korea Ministry of National Defense. 'Defense White Papers 2006-2022' *ROK MoD*

6 Joseph S. Bermudez Jr., *Shield of the Great Leader: The Armed Forces of North Korea* (St Leonards NSW: Allen & Unwin, 2001)

7 Republic of Korea Ministry of National Defense. 'Defense White Papers 2006-2022' *ROK MoD*

8 An especially important indicator would be the mobilisation of the Missile General Bureau.

9 Marine Corps Intelligence Activity. 'North Korea Country Handbook' (1997) *Federation Of American Scientists* https://fas.org/nuke/guide/dprk/nkor.pdf

10 Marine Corps Intelligence Activity. 'North Korea Country Handbook' (1997) *Federation Of American Scientists* https://fas.org/nuke/guide/dprk/nkor.pdf

11 Marine Corps Intelligence Activity. 'North Korea Country Handbook' (1997) *Federation Of American Scientists* https://fas.org/nuke/guide/dprk/nkor.pdf

12 Marine Corps Intelligence Activity. 'North Korea Country Handbook' (1997) *Federation Of American Scientists* https://fas.org/nuke/guide/dprk/nkor.pdf

13 Marine Corps Intelligence Activity. 'North Korea Country Handbook' (1997) *Federation Of American Scientists* https://fas.org/nuke/guide/dprk/nkor.pdf

Chapter 4

1 Official X page of the United States Army. https://x.com/usarmy/status/999727165800411138

2 This designation method is the source of considerable confusion, as the designation Type-64 is used for a machine gun and a pistol as well as North Korean produced ZPU-4s. Also, production dates of prototypes can predate the implied year in the designation; the first PPSh-41s were actually produced by the end of 1948.

3 Andrea Berger. *Target Markets* (Abingdon: Royal United Services Institute, 2015)

4 Conflict Armament Research. *IDENTIFYING MATERIEL MANUFACTURED IN THE DEMOCRATIC PEOPLE'S REPUBLIC OF KOREA (DPRK)* (CAR, 2023)

5 Central Intelligence Agency. 'North Korean Activities Overseas' (1984) *CIA FOIA* https://www.cia.gov/readingroom/docs/CIA-RDP85T00310R000200050003-7.pdf

6 Joby Warrick. 'A North Korean ship was seized off Egypt with a huge cache of weapons destined for a surprising buyer' (2017) *The Washington Post* https://www.washingtonpost.com/world/national-security/a-north-korean-ship-was-seized-off-egypt-with-a-huge-cache-of-weapons-destined-for-a-surprising-buyer/2017/10/01/d9a4e06e-a46d-11e7-b14f-f41773cd5a14_story.html?utm_term=.6e416b8b939a

7 Joby Warrick. 'A North Korean ship was seized off Egypt with a huge cache of weapons destined for a surprising buyer' (2017) *The Washington Post* https://www.washingtonpost.com/world/national-security/a-north-korean-ship-was-seized-off-egypt-with-a-huge-cache-of-weapons-destined-for-a-surprising-buyer/2017/10/01/d9a4e06e-a46d-11e7-b14f-f41773cd5a14_story.html?utm_term=.6e416b8b939a

8 Steve Johnson. 'North Korean PK style Belt Fed Machine Gun Found In Zimbabwe' *The Firearm Blog* (2014) https://www.thefirearmblog.com/blog/2014/08/05/north-korean-pk-style-belt-fed-machine-gun-found-zimbabwe/

9 Andrea Berger. *Target Markets* (Abingdon: Royal United Services Institute, 2015)

10 United Nations Security Council. 'Report of the Panel of Experts established pursuant to resolution 1874 (2009)' 8 March 2018 *UNSC*

11 Dan Shea and Heebum Hong. 'NORTH KOREAN SMALL ARMS' (2013) *Small Arms Defense Journal* http://www.sadefensejournal.com/wp/?p=1785

12 KCNA 'DPRK Missile Administration and Academy of Defence Sciences Make Public Important Scientific Research Achievements' (2024) KCNA Watch https://kcnawatch.org/newstream/1726701011-233356676/dprk-missile-administration-and-academy-of-defence-sciences-make-public-important-scientific-research-achievements/

13 *Mash*. 'Famous gunsmith Vladislav Lobaev has accused North Korea of stealing the development of his DVL-10 M1 "Diversant" multi-caliber silent rifle.' (2024) *Mash* https://t.me/mash/54288

14 유성운. '[천안함 폭침 1년]"北 특수부대원들 지금도 땅굴로 남한 침투"' (2011) *Dong-A Ilbo* http://news.donga.com/Politics/3/00/20110323/35801211/1

15 SaCO-Defense. 'The close combat system of the People's Army of the People's Democratic Republic of Korea (PDRK)' *SaCO-Defense* https://www.saco-defense.de/geschichte/gjogsul-de/

16 Guy M. Hicks. ' North Korea: Exporting Arms and Terror' (1984) *The Heritage Foundation* https://www.heritage.org/arms-control/report/north-korea-exporting-arms-and-terror

17 Central Intelligence Agency. 'North Korea: New Weapons For The Mechanized Forces' (1984) *CIA FOIA* https://www.cia.gov/readingroom/document/cia-rdp85t00310r000200080006-1

18 Nuclear Threat Initiative 'North Korean Missile Chronology' (2012) *NTI* https://www.nti.org/media/pdfs/north_korea_missile_2.pdf?_=1327534760?_=1327534760

19 North Korean MANPADS of any type are simplistically referred to as Hwaseong-Chong (Arquebus) in the DPRK, sometimes causing confusion amongst analysts.

20 MCLOS targeting requires the operator to track the target while simultaneously guiding the missile, usually with a joystick.

21 Oryx Blog. 'North Korean HT-16PGJ MANPADS in Syria' (2016) *Oryx Blog* https://www.oryxspioenkop.com/2016/03/north-korean-ht-16pgj-manpads-in-syria.html

22 Another batch apparently destined for Iran was intercepted in Thailand in 2009, and negotiations with Azerbaijan for the acquisition of 70 units feel through when the arms dealer involved was arrested in 2011.

23 Nuclear Threat Initiative 'North Korean Missile Chronology' (2012) *NTI* https://www.nti.org/media/pdfs/north_korea_missile_2.pdf?_=1327534760?_=1327534760

24 It appears the launcher for both variants is identical – only the missile is different, with the more modern variant carrying the designation HG-16.

25 Joseph S. Bermudez Jr., *Shield of the Great Leader: The Armed Forces of North Korea* (St Leonards NSW: Allen & Unwin, 2001)

26 The 9K111 uses wire-guided SACLOS missiles, which improve upon those utilising MCLOS due to the fact that the operator merely his to keep his sight fixated on the target to guide the missile, rather than controlling it directly.

27 Joseph S. Bermudez Jr., *Shield of the Great Leader: The Armed Forces of North Korea* (St Leonards NSW: Allen & Unwin, 2001)

28 Andrea Berger. *Target Markets* (Abingdon: Royal United Services Institute, 2015)

29 Korean Central News Agency. 'Kim Jong Un Guides Test-fire of Newly Developed Anti-tank Guided Weapon' *KCNA*

30 Oryx Blog. 'Gaza Conflict: Hamas' North Korean Arms' (2021) *Oryx Blog* https://www.oryxspioenkop.com/2021/05/gaza-conflict-hamas-north-korean-arms.html

31 Oryx Blog. 'Gaza Conflict: Hamas' North Korean Arms' (2021) *Oryx Blog* https://www.oryxspioenkop.com/2021/05/gaza-conflict-hamas-north-korean-arms.html

32 United Nations Security Council. 'Report of the Panel of Experts established pursuant to resolution 1874 (2009)' 8 March 2018 *UNSC*

33 Information obtained from the KPA Exhibition of Arms and Equipment in Pyongyang.

34 Kyodo. 'N. Korea to mass-produce Syria-provided missile' (2009) *Kyodo News* https://www.thefreelibrary.com/N.+Korea+to+mass-produce+Syria-provided+missile.-a0202321247

35 A curious device of considerably less significance was revealed in 2024, and consists of an indigenous 100mm RCL with a HEAT warhead similar to the D-10's BK-5M. Why North Korea deems it necessary to continue the development of such obsolete designs is uncertain, and it is possible that it instead concerns an older development that was only now showcased for the first time in order to demonstrate a new muzzle velocity radar.

36 Contrary to popular belief, the AK-74's magazine is actually fabricated from fiberglass-reinforced polymer (plastic), not from Bakelite.

37 This designation was invented by the authors for illustrative purposes; the North Korean designation is as of yet unknown.

38 Information obtained from Sudan's Military Industry Corporation http://mic.sd/en/home/products/

39 It is unknown if this calibre is actually manufactured in the DPRK, with a 2024 attempt to acquire 50,000 9mm rounds through a California-based Chinese smuggler suggesting this is not the case.

40 Information obtained from Glocom https://glocom-corp.com/index.php/product/detail?p=gs-2500

41 United Nations Security Council. 'Final report of the Panel of Experts submitted pursuant to resolution 2276' (2016)' 27 February 2017 UNSC.

42 GreatPoppo. 'エチオピア軍が北朝鮮起源の軍用無線機を使用している画像について' (2022) *Deep Dive* https://note.com/cccp1917/n/n86757c1d04ca

Chapter 5

1 Information obtained from the KPA Exhibition of Arms and Equipment in Pyongyang.

2 Information obtained from the KPA Exhibition of Arms and Equipment in Pyongyang.

3 Information obtained from the KPA Exhibition of Arms and Equipment in Pyongyang.

4 Central Intelligence Agency. 'NORTH KOREA: NEW WEAPONS IN THE MILITARY FORCES' (1985) *CIA FOIA* https://www.cia.gov/readingroom/document/cia-rdp85t01058r000201940001-0

5 Joost Oliemans, Stijn Mitzer 'North Korea and Ethiopia, brothers in arms' (2014) *NK News* https://www.nknews.org/2014/09/north-korean-military-support-for-ethiopia/

6 Joseph S. Bermudez Jr. 'KPA Journal Vol. 2 No.4' (2011) *KPA Journal* http://www.kpajournal.com/vol-2-no-4-april-2011/

7 The Chosun Ilbo 'N.Korea Bought Huge Numbers of Chinese Military Vehicles' (2011) *The Chosun Ilbo* http://english.chosun.com/site/data/html_dir/2011/08/23/2011082300978.html

8 Information obtained from the KPA Exhibition of Arms and Equipment in Pyongyang.

9 In the usual course of such donations, authorities instruct members of youth organisations to collect materials for munitions factories. In exchange, newly produced or refurbished military equipment is 'donated' to the KPA in the name of children.

Chapter 6

1 Mads Brügger. *The Mole: Undercover in North Korea* (2020), Wingman Media.

2 Joost Oliemans. 'Russia ups ante by deploying likely North Korean missile system for Ukraine war' (2024) NK Pro https://www.nknews.org/pro/russia-ups-ante-by-deploying-likely-north-korean-missile-system-for-ukraine-war/

ABOUT THE AUTHORS

Joost Oliemans is an analyst and author focusing on Asia, the Middle East and North Africa. Together with Stijn Mitzer, he is the author of *The Armed Forces of North Korea: On the Path of Songun*. Joost Oliemans also writes for various news agencies and websites about military-related matters.